FRANCYNE DAVIS,

a hypoglycemic or low blood sugar sufferer, freely admits that a high protein, low sugar/low carbohydrate diet can be rather boring. So she has set out with imagination and enthusiasm to put together a cookbook that not only fills the needs of over forty million of our population specifically, but caters to sophisticated palates everywhere. The culinary genius of these recipes not only fulfills dieters' and diabetics' dreams but will also excite the curiosity of the most creative cooks.

**THE LOW BLOOD
SUGAR COOKBOOK**

The Low Blood Sugar Cookbook

by Francyne Davis

Foreword by Carlton Fredericks, Ph.D.
Introduction by Marilyn Hamilton Light

BANTAM BOOKS
TORONTO · NEW YORK · LONDON

THE LOW BLOOD SUGAR COOKBOOK
A Bantam Book

PRINTING HISTORY
Grosset & Dunlap edition published March 1973
2nd printing ..... March 1973   3rd printing ...... April 1973
4th printing .... October 1973
Bantam edition / March 1974
2nd printing ..... March 1974   5th printing .... January 1976
3rd printing .... May 1974   6th printing .... January 1977
4th printing .... January 1975   7th printing ...... April 1977
8th printing ...... March 1978

ISBN 0-553-11798-X

Published simultaneously in the United States and Canada

Bantam Books are published by Bantam Books, Inc. Its trade-
mark, consisting of the words "Bantam Books" and the por-
trayal of a bantam, is registered in the United States Patent
Office and in other countries. Marca Registrada. Bantam
Books, Inc., 666 Fifth Avenue, New York, New York 10019.

PRINTED IN THE UNITED STATES OF AMERICA

Contents

For John W. Tintera

I hope this book will help those with low blood sugar realize that the diet necessary for them need not be dull, boring, or limited. There is so much to choose from and, with imagination, a world of beautiful foods that can be prepared for everyone. I want to thank Sally Markowitz for helping me take the first step into the world of publishing; Arlene Wanderman for help in the editing of the book; Ruth Siegel for being patient and able to type all my handwritten notes; Hadassah Tessler for her assistance at the stove, helping me all the way to create new recipes. To the best tasters in the world— best because they were there all the time tasting and testing—my daughter Lissa and my son Peter.

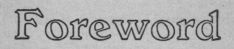

Foreword

One man's sugar is another man's poison, a statement that describes an individual difference in tolerance for foods that makes millions of people, eating the average American diet, unhappy. Bizarre as it seems, there are people who eat 125 pounds of sugar a year and yet suffer from low blood sugar. The fault, obviously, does not begin with a deficit of sugar in the diet, for the average intake may be as high as 1⅓ teaspoons of sugar every 35 minutes, 24 hours a day. The trouble begins when the body burns sugar too rapidly—a condition obviously opposite to diabetes.

The diabetic takes insulin or equivalent drugs to help him to "burn" sugar, for he produces too little of the hormone or malutilizes it. The hypoglycemic produces too *much* insulin. As a result, when he eats sugar, his pancreas is stimulated into overproducing insulin to burn the sugar. With the American penchant for sweet desserts and snacks based on sugar or starch, the hypoglycemic treads consistently on the edge of the reaction a diabetic briefly suffers when he has injected an overdose of insulin. Except that in the hypoglycemic, unlike the diabetic, the cause of the weakness, pallor, and perspiration is not often recognized.

Since the brain and the nervous system can burn no food but sugar, a deficit of the fuel is a direct threat both to the function—and, if the deficiency is pronounced enough—to the very structure of these systems. Moreover, the area of the brain that is most sensitive to a deficit of blood sugar is the emotional (thalamic) area, in which are the controls for the autonomic activities of the body—including heartbeat, breathing, and many digestive functions, among others. So it is that the sufferer with low blood sugar feels and acts like a neurotic or psychotic, with unjustified anxiety, senseless fears, claustrophobia, constant fatigue, and unprovoked depressions that may even be suicidal. Accompanying these "emotional" symptoms may be disturbances of some of the physical functions of the body which we do not ordinarily consciously control—heartbeat, pulse, breathing, digestion—with symptoms that may suggest a nonexistent ulcer, or hyperacidity, indigestion, constipation, and the like.

When you have been diagnosed as having low blood sugar, you now realize, you will be admonished to reduce your intake of sugar and starch (which the body converts into sugar). Thereby you will avoid triggering your overactive pancreas as you did in the past by eating the carbohydrates that make the blood sugar suddenly rise. At that point you will find that avoiding excessive intake of starches and learning to minimize sugar intake are not easy accomplishments, for these carbohydrates are concealed in many foods, which explains why 50 percent of the calories in the average diet are derived from such sources. Tomato catsup is full of sugar. A donut may contain five teaspoonfuls, in addition to flour, and the glazed donut supplies two teaspoonfuls more. A Danish pastry may give from 3⅓ to 6 teaspoons of sugar, a stick of chewing gum yields a half teaspoon, a bottle of soda pop (8 ounces) contains from 3½ to 5 teaspoons, a portion of cherry pie yields 14 teaspoons—and if you are indiscreet enough to take it with ice cream you now have 20 teaspoons of sugar in one portion of dessert! And when you develop indigestion from all this sugar, you buy antacid pills which themselves may be 30 percent sugar! Hence this cookbook, because you obviously need guidance in selecting menus which will provide lasting energy rather than the transient and quick rise in blood sugar which will trigger your pancreas into overreacting.

A word about individual differences in the ability to tolerate sugars and starches: even people with low blood sugar vary in the amounts of sugar and starches they can tolerate without excessive insulin production. Some people must avoid every sugar source that is avoidable, and bring their total intake of carbohydrate down to as little as 40 grams a day, or even less. Some can tolerate 60 or 100 grams of carbohydrate daily, with a very minimal amount of sugar included. Some can stand more, but none is able to remain well and function efficiently on the amount of sugar and starch represented in the average American diet. Therefore, in using this cookbook, you should begin on the assumption that you are very sensitive to sugar and somewhat sensitive to the more complex carbohydrates like starch. For the first few weeks, at least, avoid even recipes with reduced carbohydrates, such as those which specify oat flour. Once your body's management of carbohydrates is established, you may then under your doctor's supervision begin to experiment with dessert and other recipes which do contain carbohydrate.

Another individual difference centers about your

weight. A low carbohydrate diet becomes a reducing diet if margarine is substituted for butter in recipes that call for the latter. Such a substitution may be made on a spoon-for-spoon basis. When weight loss is desired the quantity of margarine and salad oil in the daily low-carbohydrate menu should together approximate 5 teaspoonfuls. The same standard for this type of fat should be exercised if your physician, while treating your low blood sugar, also wishes to help keep your blood cholesterol from rising.

Decaffeinated coffee is mentioned in this book as a beverage and a flavoring agent in certain recipes. No hypoglycemic should use ordinary coffee in any form. Most will tolerate decaffeinated coffee. A small number will find even the small amount of caffeine left in such coffee to be intolerable. If this puzzles you, the intolerance arises because caffeine gives you a lift by stimulating the liver into releasing stored sugar. When that reaches the blood, it will trigger the pancreas into releasing insulin, exactly as a sweet dessert will. Generally speaking, a hypoglycemic in the first 4 to 6 weeks will do well to avoid all forms of coffee and tea, chocolate, cocoa, and cola drinks.

The intake of protein and Vitamin B complex is very important to liver function, which in turn, is as vital to the body's management of blood sugar as is the pancreas. To fortify your intake of the Vitamin B complex, it will be well to employ two teaspoons of wheat germ in every cup of flour recommended in the recipes in this hypoglycemia cookbook. It will also serve you well to supplement your diet with brewer's yeast and desiccated liver, and to include such organ meats as liver in your menus.

Remember that for a hypoglycemic the timing of his meals is as critical as their content. Ideally, eat six times a day—not more food, but more frequently. We don't want blood sugar curves that look like a hairpin —rapidly rising, triggering the pancreas, and thereby rapidly falling. This is a chicken-to-feathers-to-chicken type of existence. We want a more gentle rise and a more gentle fall in blood-sugar levels, which will make for better function of the nervous system and brain and heightened well-being for you. This is a great understatement of the benefits hypoglycemics enjoy when their foods follow the pattern of the recipes you find in this cookbook. As one physician put it, there is no need for these people to be tired, nervous wrecks. But these are not the only possible dividends from a low-sugar, low-starch type of diet for those who need it— because sugar is blamed for tooth decay, indicated as a contributor to hardening of the arteries, and helps to create liver disturbances which may contribute to the pain, tension, and nervousness which women believe to be normal to the menstrual cycle. For those who retain salt when they eat these carbohydrates, such menus will often contribute to sudden and dramatic weight losses. In short, this is more than a cookbook— it is a way of life.

CARLTON FREDERICKS,
Ph.D.

Introduction

What is hypoglycemia? Hypoglycemia is defined as "a condition produced by a low level of glucose in the blood" (Gould's *Medical Dictionary*).

You may wonder of what significance this is to you. First, you should know that the brain is nourished *exclusively* by glucose. You can readily understand, therefore, that a constant, adequate amount of glucose is absolutely necessary for proper function—*your* proper function. If your blood sugar falls too low you may feel confused, you may have headaches, visual disturbances, weakness, sweating, rapid beating of the heart, anxiety, nervousness, tremor, and hunger.

Think about it. You may have dashed off to your office this morning with only a cup of coffee and a piece of toast for breakfast. About ten o'clock you begin to feel tired, lightheaded, you can't concentrate, and what do you do? You have another cup of coffee "to pick you up." Or you may be in school and around ten o'clock you feel depressed, picked on, can't concentrate in class. If instead you had had a breakfast of eggs, bacon, fruit, milk, and a piece of low-carbohydrate toast, you would probably feel fine and alert and able to function beautifully and efficiently until lunchtime.

What would cause the feeling of well-being from the good breakfast? You would have had sufficient good quality protein and no readily available carbohydrate; your blood sugar would have risen to normal, returned to around fasting level, and stayed there until lunchtime.

What are the mechanics of all of this? You have a cup of coffee and toast and your blood sugar jumps up quickly, *but* it cannot be maintained. You have stimulated your pancreas to produce insulin (the substance for dealing with blood sugar). Your blood sugar has shot up and insulin is produced to deal with it. Then the adrenal gland is called upon to antagonize the insulin reaction and prevent the blood sugar from falling too low. This is the normal reaction to ingestion of food. When constant triggering to overresponse is created through poor eating habits, this normal reaction becomes abnormal—too much insulin reaction, too little adrenal cortical response. The result: hypoglycemia, low blood sugar.

Let's consider the background. Dr. Seale Harris described patients who had symptoms of overdose of insulin without having taken insulin. From his work, it became clear that people can and do react inappropriately to carbohydrate and this problem can be controlled by proper diet, a diet high in protein, low in carbohydrate.

You may ask, what are proteins? What are carbohydrates? Protein comes from the Greek *protos,* or first. It might be said protein is "of first importance." Proteins are meats, poultry, fish and seafood. The purpose of protein is the maintenance and repair of the body. Without adequate protein, the body is weakened and repair is retarded. You can readily see that this substance, protein, is "of first importance."

What are carbohydrates? Carbohydrates are in those foods which we all like: vegetables, fruits, grains and sugars.

Let's consider what has been said about carbohydrates by Samuel Soskin, M.D. and R. Levine, M.D. ("The Role of Carbohydrates in the Diet," *Dietotherapy Clinical Application of Modern Nutrition,* pp. 42-43).

"Though there has been some change during the past fifty years in the food sources from which the carbohydrates are derived, the proportion of carbohydrate in the dietary of the United States has remained about 50-60 percent of the total caloric intake. Since certain foods high in carbohydrate content are relatively inexpensive, the proportion of carbohydrate in the diet has been greater at lower economic levels than in the more prosperous groups of the population. The poorer nutritional status of the lowest income groups, however, is not so much a reflection of their high carbohydrate intake as it is a result of the particular foods from which they derive their carbohydrates. The highly refined grains and sugars, developed commercially largely because of their resistance to spoilage are the cheapest sources of calories generally available. But they have been deprived of most of the protective elements with which they are naturally endowed; hence a *casually selected* high-carbohydrate diet is likely to be poor in the essential amino acids, vitamins and minerals."

What does all this mean in connection with hypoglycemia? Simply, refined carbohydrates (sugars, starches) provide a quick "pickup" without providing good nutrition. Sugar, as we know it, is eaten and does not require complex handling by the body to be effective. You by-pass normal body function by eating sugars and refined foods. For the person who has hypoglycemia, these foods provide the "trigger" for a hypoglycemic episode. For the so-called normal person, nothing is provided but a pickup with no nutritional benefit and the potential of disturbing the mechanism for proper handling of food.

The diet to prevent hypoglycemia is high in protein and low in carbohydrates. All "highly refined" carbohydrates are eliminated from the diet. Meals are planned around protein foods, meats, fish, poultry, and cheese, with vegetables and fruits added.

Cakes, refined cereals, breads, pastries, candies, pies . . . all the so-called good things we like to eat are eliminated from the diet to prevent hypoglycemia and to insure efficient function.

If you consider that only in recent years, perhaps since the beginning of the twentieth century, it has been the rule rather than the exception to eat such foods (cakes, cokes, pies, etc.) daily, you will see the course nutrition has taken. In the past, these "good" foods were reserved for occasions: weddings, holidays and other celebrations. Today, every day is a "celebration" and the celebration is at the expense of good nutrition and normal function.

Volumes have been written about the overfed, obese American and his tendency to heart disease, high blood pressure and diabetes, all obviously problems directly related to eating habits. Our daily celebrations are the culprits.

Mrs. Davis has written this book to provide recipes which are suitable for the person who has hypoglycemia. The recipes provide excellent nutrition and include dishes which are "celebrations." These celebrations serve to satisfy our American taste for the good things, but are, at the same time, good food and good nutrition.

This is a cookbook for persons who have hypoglycemia. This is a book for YOU. This is a cookbook for "normal" people who want to eat to provide nutrition which will serve every need and most particularly will prevent any possible lack of efficiency because of low blood sugar. We work with our brains and let our highly mechanized civilization work for us. If we are the "brains" then we must have brains that are able to function. This can be accomplished by selecting a diet which is suitable for efficient brain work . . . high protein, low carbohydrate. "Man does not live by bread alone" might better be stated: Man does not live by bread! The American breakfast of toast, a sweet roll and coffee provides little protein and certainly does not insure that you will be an alert, efficient "brain," functioning beautifully whether you are in the office, schoolroom, factory, or home.

Nutrition in recent years has been unfortunately confused by labels such as "faddism." Good nutrition is not faddism; it is good sense! This book offers to you an adventure . . . an adventure that promises exciting rewards: efficient repair of the body and efficient function of the brain. Mrs. Davis has prepared this book as her gift to all persons who have hypoglycemia and to all who seek good nutrition.

Today there are endless articles about the environmental difficulties of our civilization: air pollution, chemical pollution, and the like. These are huge problems which require the cooperation of us all. We, as individuals, however, have in our hands the solution to one problem. We can eat properly and hedge the bet against the environmental conditions we cannot personally control.

I urge that you accept Mrs. Davis' gift and start on the adventure to good nutrition, efficiency and a vital living!

MARILYN HAMILTON LIGHT

Executive Director,
Adrenal Metabolic Research Society
of the Hypoglycemia Foundation
Mount Vernon, New York

General
Dietary
Program

Allowable Proteins

Meat, Fowl, Fish, Shellfish

Excellent sources of protein. Serve ¼ pound or more for meals; ⅛ pound for snack. Read labels carefully.

Cheese, Dairy Products, Eggs

Excellent source of protein. Cream cheese and cottage cheese have roughly half the protein value of most other cheeses.

Nuts

Good source of protein:

pignolia nuts	pumpkin or squash kernels
butternuts	black walnuts
Brazil nuts	pecan nuts
	peanuts

Allowable Vegetables

3 percent Carbohydrate	*6 percent Carbohydrate*
beet greens	asparagus
celery	bamboo shoots
chicory	bean sprouts
Chinese cabbage	broccoli
chives	cabbage, raw
cucumbers	cauliflower
endive	chard
escarole	collard greens, raw
fennel	dandelion greens
lettuce	eggplant
olives	kale
parsley	leeks
dill and sour pickles	mustard greens
poke	mushrooms
radishes	okra
watercress	green onions
	peppers
	pimentos
	peas, edible pod
	sauerkraut
	spinach
	summer squash
	tomato
	turnip
	turnip greens
	water chestnuts
	zucchini

Allowable Vegetables

10 percent Carbohydrate	*15 percent Carbohydrate*
artichoke, globe or French	(should not be used with
beans, green or wax	10% bread, gravy,
carrots	breaded meats or fruit)
celeriac	beets
cabbage, cooked	parsnips
Brussels sprouts	peas
collard greens, cooked	pumpkin
chervil	salsify
garden cress	soybeans
kohlrabi	squash, Hubbard or winter
onion, raw	artichoke, spaghetti and
rutabaga	macaroni (if allowed by
tomato puree	physician)

Allowable Fruits

7 percent Carbohydrate	*15 percent Carbohydrate*
avocado	apples
rhubarb	apricots
	blackberries
10 percent Carbohydrate	blueberries
boysenberries	cherries
cantaloupe	dewberries
casaba melon	elderberries
coconut, fresh	grapefruit
cranberries, raw	loganberries
fruit salad (no grapes)	oranges
gooseberries	peaches
honeydew melon	pears
lemon	pineapple
lime	plums
muskmelon	raspberries
strawberries	tangerine
	youngberries

Note: Although bananas contain 23% carbohydrate, some physicians allow up to two small bananas per week, spread in small amounts through the week, taken with protein, because of the high potassium content. Recommended only on physician's advice.

Allowable Beverages

No Carbohydrate
artificially sweetened
　carbonated soft drinks
　(no cola)
clear broth
herb teas
decaffeinated coffee, if
　tolerated
weak tea, if tolerated

*5 percent Carbohydrate
gm per ½ cup*
sauerkraut juice
tomato juice
V-8 juice
vegetable juice
milk

*10 percent Carbohydrate
gm per ½ cup*
blackberry juice
carrot juice
lemon
lime
pomegranate

*15 percent Carbohydrate
gm per ½ cup*
apricot juice (not nectar)
grapefruit juice
loganberry juice
orange juice
pineapple juice
raspberry juice
tangerine juice

Bread, Crackers, Flour, etc.—
only as allowed by physician

No more than three slices a day (or the equivalent) of protein bread or crackers made of oat, soya, high gluten, and/or Jerusalem artichoke flours. Do not serve more than one slice at any one time. Not to be served with gravy (using any of the above flours), breaded meats, heavy sauce, 15 percent vegetables, or if desserts are included in the menu.

Condiments

All condiments are allowed. On prepared relishes, pickles, dressings, ketchup, mayonnaise, bouillon, soup, sauce, mustard, etc., carefully check labels for sugar or starch.

Artificial Sweeteners—if tolerated

Note: Sorbitol and mannitol are used in many products labeled as dietetic. These are generally not well tolerated by hypoglycemics, and, unless otherwise specified by your physician, should be avoided.

Fats

The use of butter, cream, whole milk (if tolerated), and salad oil is necessary to obtain a well-balanced diet, in addition to the fats naturally present in other foods in the diet.

Foods to Avoid

Beverages
alcoholic beverages
caffeine drinks
cocoa—sweetened
coffee
cola drinks
grape juice
Ovaltine
papaya juice
Postum
prune juice
soft drinks
strong tea

Vegetables
barley
corn and corn products
dried beans and peas
hominy
potatoes
rice
shell beans (lima and others)
sweet pickles
sweet relishes
sweet potatoes
yams

Fruits
dried fruits
fruits canned in syrup
grapes
guava
huckleberries
mango
plantain

Meats
*canned meat
*cold cuts
*hot dogs
*salami
*sausages
  scrapple

Pasta
macaroni
matzoh meal
noodles
spaghetti

Breads
bread
cereal
crackers
grits
matzoh
pancakes
pizza

rolls
waffles

Desserts
cake
cashew nuts
chestnuts
chewing gum
chocolate—sweetened
cookies
custards
dessert toppings
ice cream
Jell-O
pastry
pie
potato chips
pretzels
puddings

Sweets
candy
caramel
honey
jam
jelly
malt
marmalade
molasses
sugar
syrup

Dextrose, fructose, glucose, hexitol, lactose, maltose, mannitol, sorbitol, sucrose are all forms of sugar and

---

* Usually packed with some form of sugar as preservative. Check labels for exceptions.

are not allowed when used in the form of artificial sweetener.

Most canned soups and juices, ketchups, mayonnaise, mustard, salad dressings, and some canned vegetables contain sugar or starch. Read labels carefully.

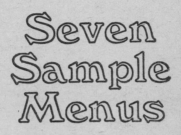

Seven
Sample
Menus

Note: Choice of beverages includes milk, weak tea, instant or percolated decaffeinated coffee.

Breakfast	Snack
½ grapefruit 1 poached egg Slice of broiled ham Beverage	Plain yogurt

Lunch	Snack
Beef pattie Sliced tomato and salad greens—dressing Fresh or stewed fruit Beverage	1 ounce cheese

Dinner	Snack

Broiled salmon steak
   (broil one extra portion
   for tomorrow)
Green beans with mush-
   rooms
Cauliflower au gratin
Sponge cake
Beverage
	4 ounces milk

Breakfast	*Snack*
½ cantaloupe ⅓ cup oatmeal 2–3 slices bacon Beverage	2 ounces cold sliced meat

Lunch	*Snack*
Cheese omelet Green salad—dressing Fresh or stewed fruit Beverage	Salmon steak (extra portion broiled yesterday)

Dinner	*Snack*
Hearty beef stew Green salad— dressing Pineapple–apricot freeze Beverage	4 ounces milk Sponge cake

Breakfast	*Snack*

4 ounces orange juice
2 scrambled eggs
Slice broiled ham
1 slice allowed bread,
    toasted
Beverage
	Yogurt mixed with
	    water-packed fruit

Lunch	*Snack*
Leftover beef stew Green salad—dressing Beverage	1 ounce nuts

Dinner	*Snack*
Barbecued chicken Braised red cabbage Riced carrots Walnut roll Beverage	4 ounces milk

Breakfast	*Snack*
4 ounces unsweetened grapefruit juice Omelet 2 slices bacon Beverage	Barbecued chicken (from last night's dinner) 4 ounces milk

Lunch	*Snack*
Tuna fish salad—mayon- naise dressing Sliced tomato, sliced cu- cumber, lettuce Fresh or stewed fruit Beverage	Walnut roll

Dinner	*Snack*
4 ounces tomato juice Broiled liver Mashed turnips Broiled eggplant slices Party chocolate loaf Beverage	Milk shake

Breakfast	*Snack*
4 ounces unsweetened pineapple juice Slice broiled ham 1 fried egg 1 slice allowed bread, toasted Beverage	4 ounces cottage cheese—½ apple

Lunch	*Snack*
Shrimp plate Avocado and lettuce salad —dressing Beverage	Yogurt spiced with cinnamon and nutmeg

Dinner	*Snack*
Italian meatloaf Brussels sprouts Parsnips Baked custard Beverage	Slice banana cake Weak tea

Breakfast	*Snack*
4 ounces orange juice 2 scrambled eggs Broiled sausage Beverage	Slice leftover meatloaf

Lunch	*Snack*
Sardines and green salad— dressing Slice banana cake Beverage	Cheddar cheese and apple cubes

Dinner

Broiled loin lamb chops
  Parmesan
Artichoke spaghetti—
  tomato sauce
Mixed salad—dressing
Fresh or stewed fruit

Snack

4 ounces milk
2 peanut butter cookies

Breakfast

4 ounces orange juice
3 soy pancakes
2 slices bacon
Beverage

Snack

Celery ribs stuffed with
  cheese

Lunch

Small can salmon
Green salad—dressing
Fresh or stewed fruit
Beverage

Snack

4 ounces milk
2 peanut butter cookies

Dinner

Roast beef
Baked summer squash
Stewed tomatoes
One small baked potato
  (if allowed)
Vanilla ice cream
Beverage

Snack

4 ounces milk
Mom's apple pie

Spreads
and
Dips

BLUE CHEESE EGG SPREAD

(Makes about 2 cups)

6 hard-cooked eggs, sieved

2 ounces blue cheese, crumbled

2 teaspoons onion salt

½ cup sour cream

In a bowl, combine eggs, cheese, onion salt, and sour cream. Beat until smooth. Consistency should be soft enough to permit spreading. Chill thoroughly for blending of flavors. Before spreading, beat dip slightly to fluff and soften.

LIPTAUER

½ pound butter

½ pound cream cheese

1 tablespoon caraway seeds

2 tablespoons minced onion

1 tablespoon anchovy paste

1½ tablespoons paprika

1 tablespoon chopped capers

In a bowl, cream butter and cheese. Add remaining ingredients. Mix well. Form into small balls and refrigerate. Serve on cocktail picks.

PARTY EGG SPREAD

(Makes about 3 cups)

8 hard-cooked eggs, riced or sieved	2 teaspoons lemon juice
1½ cups sour cream	1 teaspoon salt
2 teaspoons finely chopped onion	¼ teaspoon cayenne pepper
¼ cup chopped parsley	3 drops Tabasco

In a bowl, combine all ingredients. Beat until smooth. Refrigerate until ready to spread on slices of allowed bread.

PEANUT BUTTER

(Makes 1 cup)

1 cup freshly roasted peanuts	3 tablespoons peanut oil
	Salt to taste

Combine nuts and oil in a blender container. Cover blender and blend until mixture is smooth. Add salt. Store in a jar with a tightly fitted cover.

SUSAN ABBOTT'S CURRY DIP

(Makes about 1 cup)

⅓ cup mayonnaise	Curry powder to taste
⅔ cup sour cream	Lemon juice to taste

Blend all ingredients in a bowl. Chill and serve with cold shrimp or cold raw vegetables.

SUSAN ABBOTT'S LIPTAUER

(Makes about 1½ cups)

1½ sticks butter, softened	2 tablespoons grated onion
½ pound cream cheese, softened	2 tablespoons chopped capers
½ tube anchovy paste	

In a bowl, cream butter and cheese. Add anchovy paste, onion and capers. Blend thoroughly. Serve with cucumber slices, cherry tomatoes, radishes, celery ribs and cauliflowerettes.

SUSAN ABBOTT'S SOUR CREAM DILL DIP

(Makes about 1½ cups)

½ cup sour cream	Lemon juice to taste
½ cup mayonnaise	Salt to taste
1 large bunch of fresh dill, snipped	

In a blender container, combine sour cream, mayonnaise and dill. Cover and blend until dill is finely chopped. Add lemon juice and salt. Refrigerate until ready to serve.

Breads
and
Pancakes

THE BREAD

(Makes 1 loaf)

6 eggs, separated

1 tablespoon caraway seeds

½ teaspoon salt

1 cup soy flour, sifted

Preheat oven to 350 degrees F.

In a bowl, beat egg yolks until very thick and lemon-colored. Add salt and caraway seeds. Beat egg whites until stiff. Fold egg yolks into stiffly beaten egg whites. Sift soy flour over egg mixture. Fold in carefully. Pour mixture into a buttered 5¼-inch x 9½-inch bread pan. Bake 25 minutes. Reduce heat to 250 degrees F. and continue to bake for 15 minutes more. Cool, slice and serve.

OAT MUFFINS

(Makes 6–8 muffins)

1 cup sifted oat flour	1 egg, well beaten
⅛ teaspoon salt	¼ cup cold water
2½ teaspoons baking powder	2 tablespoons melted butter
8 drops noncaloric liquid sweetener	

Preheat oven to 425 degrees F.

In a bowl, combine oat flour, salt and baking powder. Add liquid sweetener, egg and water. Mix until smooth. Stir in butter. Pour into buttered muffin tins. Bake for 25 minutes.

PINWHEELS

(Makes 8–10)

Prepare batter for "The Bread" (page 27)	4 tablespoons sour cream
	6 ounces red caviar
1 package (3 ounces) cream cheese, softened	½ teaspoon finely chopped onion

Preheat oven to 350 degrees F.

Oil a jelly-roll pan. Line it with waxed paper. Oil the paper and spoon the prepared batter into the prepared pan. Bake for 12-15 minutes. Invert the pan onto a towel. Remove pan and peel off paper. Roll towel and bread. Cool. In a bowl, combine cream cheese, sour cream, caviar and onion. Spread mixture evenly on the cooled roll. Roll up and chill for 1 hour. Cut roll into ¼-inch slices and arrange on a serving plate.

DUMPLINGS

(Makes 6–8 servings)

1 cup oat flour   Pinch of salt
1 cup pot cheese   Boiling salted water
1 egg

In a bowl, combine all ingredients except water. Mix thoroughly. Refrigerate mixture until chilled. Break off pieces the size of a walnut. Roll gently between palms. Drop carefully into the boiling water. Cook for 5 minutes. Remove dumplings, using a slotted spoon. Serve with stew, goulash or pot roast.

GRIDDLE CAKES

(Makes 2–3 servings)

1 egg, lightly beaten   1½ teaspoons baking
2 tablespoons salad oil   powder
½ cup milk   ¼ teaspoon salt
½ cup oat flour   Few drops noncaloric
                                  liquid sweetener

In a bowl, combine egg, salad oil and milk. Add remaining ingredients. Combine thoroughly. Cook by spoonfuls on a hot griddle until browned on both sides.

COTTAGE CHEESE PANCAKES

(Makes 10–12 pancakes)

3 eggs, well beaten   ¼ cup oat flour
1 cup cottage cheese   ½ teaspoon salt
2 tablespoons salad oil

Combine all ingredients in a bowl. Blend thoroughly.
Cook by spoonfuls on a hot griddle until browned on
both sides.

SOY PANCAKES

(Makes 8–9 pancakes)

1 egg, slightly beaten   ½ cup soy flour, sifted
2 tablespoons salad oil   ¼ cup oat flour, sifted
½ cup milk   1½ teaspoons baking
1 teaspoon salt   powder

In a bowl, combine egg, salad oil and milk. Mix thoroughly. Add dry ingredients and stir to blend. Cook by
spoonfuls on a hot griddle until browned on one side.
Turn pancake and cook until browned on other side.
Serve with hot melted butter and your favorite fruit
concentrate syrup.

CREPES

(Makes about 8 crêpes)

2 eggs, slightly beaten   ⅓ cup milk
⅓ cup oat flour   ⅓ cup water
¼ teaspoon salt   Salad oil

In a bowl, combine all ingredients, except oil. Stir until batter is smooth. Let batter stand for 1 hour. Heat

a 7-inch skillet or crêpe pan until hot. Lightly brush bottom of pan with salad oil. Pour in a generous tablespoon of batter. Quickly tilt pan so that batter covers bottom of pan evenly. Cook for 1 minute or until bottom of crêpe is cooked. Lift crêpe and turn over. Cook other side until done. Stack finished crêpes until ready to use. Crêpes may be frozen.

TUNA-FILLED CREPES

(Makes 3–4 servings)

Filling

1 can (3¼ ounces) tuna fish, drained	½ teaspoon grated onion
2 hard-cooked eggs, finely chopped	3 artichoke bottoms, chopped
¼ teaspoon salt	½ cup sour cream
	9 7-inch crêpes

Preheat oven to 400 degrees F.

In a bowl, break up tuna fish with a fork. Add eggs, salt, onion, artichoke bottoms and sour cream. Blend thoroughly. Place 1 heaping tablespoon of mixture on each crêpe. Roll up into thirds. Place in a buttered shallow baking dish, seam side down. Top with cheese sauce. Bake for 15–20 minutes, or until sauce is bubbly.

Cheese Sauce

2 tablespoons butter	2 ounces Swiss cheese, cubed
2 tablespoons oat flour	Salt to taste
1 cup milk	

Melt butter in a saucepan. Stir in oat flour. Cook for 2 minutes, stirring constantly. Add milk and continue cooking over low heat, stirring until sauce bubbles. Add cheese. Cook until cheese melts. Season with salt.

VEGETABLE CREPES

(Makes 3–4 servings)

¼ cup bean sprouts, canned or fresh
¼ cup thinly sliced celery
¼ cup sliced scallions
¼ cup shredded cabbage
¼ cup thinly sliced green pepper
6 mushrooms, sliced
2 tablespoons salad oil
Salt to taste
Pepper to taste
Salad oil
9 7-inch crêpes

In a saucepan, combine vegetables and 2 tablespoons salad oil. Cook for 15 minutes, stirring occasionally. Add salt and pepper. Place a heaping tablespoonful of mixture on each crêpe. Roll up into thirds. Heat oil in a heavy skillet. Sauté crêpes until lightly browned on both sides.

AILENE'S MANICOTTI

(Makes 3–4 servings)

¾ pound Ricotta cheese
½ pound Mozzarella cheese, diced
3 tablespoons chopped parsley
Salt to taste
Pepper to taste
3 cups tomato sauce
¼ cup grated Parmesan cheese
9 7-inch crêpes

Preheat oven to 350 degrees F.

In a bowl, combine Ricotta cheese, Mozzarella cheese, parsley, salt and pepper. Fill center of each crêpe with mixture. Fold into thirds. Place crêpes in a baking dish and spoon over tomato sauce. Sprinkle with Parmesan cheese. Bake for 25 minutes or until sauce bubbles.

PROSCIUTTO-CHEESE CREPES

(Makes 3–4 servings)

¼ cup diced Mozza-
rella cheese
¼ cup grated Parme-
san cheese

½ cup chopped
Prosciutto ham
9 7-inch crêpes
½ cup hot tomato
sauce

Preheat oven to 325 degrees F.

In a bowl, combine cheeses and ham. Place a heaping tablespoon in center of each crêpe. Roll up into thirds. Place crêpes, seam side down, in a shallow baking dish. Pour over the hot sauce. Bake for 15 minutes.

DESSERT CREPES

(Makes about 8 crêpes)

2 eggs, slightly beaten
⅓ cup oat flour, sifted
6 drops noncaloric
liquid sweetener

⅓ cup milk
⅓ cup water
Melted butter

In a bowl, combine eggs, oat flour, and liquid sweetener. Add milk and water, stirring until batter is smooth (it will be thin). Let batter stand for 1 hour. Heat a 7-inch skillet or crêpe pan until hot. Lightly brush bottom of pan with melted butter. Pour in a generous tablespoon of batter. Quickly rotate pan so the batter covers the bottom of pan evenly. Cook for 1 minute, or until bottom of crêpe is cooked. Lift crêpe carefully and turn it over. Cook other side for about 30 seconds, or until crêpe is done. Stack finished crêpes until ready to use. Crêpes may be frozen.

APPLE AND WALNUT BLINTZES (CREPES)

(Makes 3–4 servings)

¾ cup finely chopped
apples

⅛ teaspoon ground
ginger

⅛ teaspoon nutmeg

1 tablespoon melted
butter

¼ cup finely chopped
walnuts

Noncaloric liquid
sweetener to taste

9 7-inch crêpes

Butter

Sour cream

In a bowl, combine apples, ginger, nutmeg, melted butter, walnuts and liquid sweetener. Place a tablespoonful of mixture in center of each crêpe. Roll into thirds. Melt butter in a heavy skillet. Sauté crêpes until browned on both sides. Top each crêpe with a dollop of sour cream.

CHEESE BLINTZES (CREPES)

(Makes 3–4 servings)

½ cup cottage cheese

1 package (3 ounces)
cream cheese

1 tablespoon sour
cream

1 egg yolk, slightly
beaten

¾ teaspoon noncaloric
liquid sweetener

¼ teaspoon salt

¾ teaspoon grated
lemon rind

9 7-inch crêpes

3 tablespoons butter

In a bowl, combine cheeses. Blend thoroughly. Add sour cream, egg yolk, liquid sweetener, salt and lemon rind. Mix well. Place a heaping tablespoon of mixture in center of each crêpe. Roll up into thirds. In a large skillet, melt butter. Sauté blintzes until browned on both sides.

BLUEBERRY BLINTZES

(Makes 3–4 servings)

1 cup blueberries, washed and dried

1¼ teaspoons non-caloric liquid sweetener

¼ teaspoon lemon rind

9 7-inch crêpes

Butter

In a bowl, combine blueberries, liquid sweetener and lemon rind. Place a heaping tablespoon of mixture in center of each crêpe. Fold into thirds. Sauté in butter until browned on both sides.

PEACH BLINTZES (CREPES)

(Makes 4 servings)

¾ cup finely chopped peaches

3 teaspoons non-caloric liquid sweetener

⅛ teaspoon ground ginger

1 egg white, stiffly beaten

8 7-inch crêpes

3 tablespoons melted butter

Preheat oven to 400 degrees F.

In a bowl, combine peaches, 2 teaspoons liquid sweetener, and ginger. Fold mixture into stiffly beaten egg white. Place a heaping tablespoon of mixture in center of each crêpe. Fold into thirds. Place in a buttered baking pan. Sprinkle with melted butter and remaining liquid sweetener. Bake for 10 minutes.

PINEAPPLE-CHEESE BLINTZES (CREPES)

(Makes 3–4 servings)

1 egg yolk, lightly
    beaten
½ teaspoon noncaloric
    liquid sweetener
½ cup cottage cheese

½ cup crushed
    unsweetened pine-
    apple, drained
¼ teaspoon grated
    lemon rind
9 7-inch crêpes
3 tablespoons butter

In a bowl, combine egg yolk, liquid sweetener and cottage cheese. Beat until smooth. Add pineapple and
lemon rind. Mix thoroughly. Place a spoonful of mixture in center of each crêpe. Roll into thirds. Melt butter in a heavy skillet. Sauté until lightly browned on
both sides.

STRAWBERRY-CHEESE CREPES

(Makes 4 servings)

½ cup sliced
    strawberries
½ cup cottage cheese
¾ teaspoon noncaloric
    liquid sweetener

8 7-inch crêpes
3 tablespoons butter
Sour cream

In a bowl, combine strawberries, cottage cheese and
liquid sweetener. Place about 1½ tablespoons of filling
in the center of each crêpe. Fold into thirds. Melt butter in a heavy skillet. Add crêpes and cook until golden
brown on each side. Serve immediately with a dollop
of sour cream on top of each crêpe.

WALNUT BLINTZES

(Makes about 9 blintzes)

Blintzes
¼ cup cold water
1 teaspoon noncaloric liquid sweetener
1 teaspoon walnut extract
1 teaspoon vanilla extract

3 eggs, lightly beaten
1½ tablespoons oat flour
6 tablespoons grated walnuts
2 tablespoons butter, melted

In a bowl, combine all ingredients and beat thoroughly. Lightly brush bottom of a hot 7-inch skillet with butter. Pour a tablespoon of batter into skillet, rotating pan to cover bottom evenly. Cook on both sides until light brown. Fill crêpes and roll up. Sauté in additional butter until hot. Serve with sour cream as garnish.

Filling
3 tablespoons spiced applesauce, unsweetened

3 tablespoons cottage cheese

Combine ingredients and mix thoroughly. Allow 2 tablespoons of filling for each crêpe.

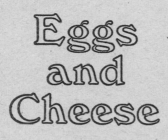

Eggs and Cheese

PLAIN OMELET

(Makes 1 serving)

2 eggs
2 tablespoons cold
  water

¼ teaspoon salt
⅛ teaspoon pepper
1 tablespoon butter

In a bowl, combine eggs, water, salt and pepper. Mix well with a wire whisk or fork. Do not overbeat. Heat butter in a 7-inch skillet or omelet pan hot enough to sizzle a drop of water. Pour in egg mixture. With a spatula or fork, draw cooked portions at edges toward center, so that uncooked portions flow to bottom. Slide pan back and forth over heat to keep mixture in motion and avoid sticking. When mixture is set and eggs are still moist, increase heat to brown bottom quickly. Lift the side nearest the skillet handle and fold about ⅓ of omelet over center. Slide omelet toward outside of skillet and fold the outer edge over the center. Slide omelet onto a warm plate. Serve immediately.

COTTAGE CHEESE OMELET

(Makes 6 servings)

6 eggs, separated	Salt to taste
1 cup cottage cheese	Pepper to taste
¾ cup light cream	2 tablespoons butter
3 tablespoons finely chopped parsley	

Preheat oven to 350 degrees F.

In a bowl, combine egg yolks, cheese, cream, parsley, salt and pepper. Blend well. In another bowl, beat egg whites until stiff. Fold into egg yolk mixture. In a heavy skillet, melt butter. Add mixture and cook over low heat until the bottom is golden brown. Remove skillet from range and place in oven. Bake for 15–20 minutes, or until the top is golden brown. Serve immediately.

EGG FOO YONG

(Makes 4 servings)

5 eggs	1 tablespoon soy sauce
1 cup bean sprouts	½ cup cooked meat or fish, shredded
½ cup celery, thinly sliced	1 teaspoon salt
¼ cup onion, thinly sliced	¼ teaspoon mono-sodium glutamate
¼ pound mushrooms, thinly sliced	⅛ teaspoon pepper
	Vegetable oil

In a bowl, combine all ingredients, except vegetable oil. Mix well. Heat oil in a large, heavy skillet. Using a ladle, drop mixture into hot oil. Fry omelets until browned on both sides. Remove and serve hot.

CHEDDAR CHEESE OMELET

(Makes 4 servings)

4 eggs, slightly beaten
¼ teaspoon salt
6 tablespoons milk

1 cup Cheddar cheese, shredded
4 tablespoons butter

In a bowl, combine eggs, salt, milk and cheese. Mix thoroughly. Melt butter in a 10-inch omelet pan. Pour in the egg mixture. Cover the pan. Cook over very low heat for 15 minutes, or until bottom of omelet is lightly browned. Fold omelet in half. Serve immediately.

TUNA TIME OMELET FILLING

(Makes 4 servings)

1 can (7 ounces) water-packed tuna, drained and flaked
2 tablespoons finely chopped green pepper
2 tablespoons mayonnaise

1 tablespoon lemon juice
1 teaspoon onion powder
½ teaspoon salt
4 omelets (see recipe page 41)

In a bowl, combine tuna fish, green pepper, mayonnaise, lemon juice, onion powder and salt. Set aside. Prepare each omelet. Before folding, place ¼ of tuna mixture on half of omelet. Fold omelet over tuna mixture and slide hot omelet onto plate.

ST. PATRICK'S DAY OMELET

(Makes 4 servings)

2 packages (3 ounces each) cream cheese, softened
2½ teaspoons chopped chives
4 eggs, separated
2½ tablespoons light cream
1 teaspoon salt
⅛ teaspoon pepper
3 tablespoons butter

Preheat oven to 325 degrees F.

In a bowl, combine cream cheese and chives. Add egg yolks, one at a time, beating well after each addition. Add cream and seasonings. Beat egg whites until stiff. Fold into the egg yolk mixture. In a heavy skillet, melt butter. Pour in mixture. Cook over low heat until bottom begins to brown. Transfer skillet to oven. Cook until top of omelet is dry. Fold the omelet. Serve immediately.

EGGS WITH TOMATOES AND PEPPER

(Makes 3 servings)

6 tablespoons butter
3 green peppers, thinly sliced
1 large onion, thinly sliced
1 clove garlic, crushed
3 small tomatoes
Salt to taste
Pepper to taste
5 eggs
¼ cup heavy cream

In a saucepan, melt 3 tablespoons butter. Add peppers and onion. Sauté until tender. Add tomatoes, garlic, salt and pepper. Simmer vegetables until they are soft. Set aside. In a bowl, beat eggs lightly with cream. In a large skillet, melt remaining butter. Add eggs and cook over low heat, stirring constantly, until eggs are set. To serve, place eggs on a warm platter and surround with hot cooked vegetables.

BAKED EGGS PROSCIUTTO

(Makes 2 servings)

4 eggs	2 slices Prosciutto
2 tablespoons grated	ham, chopped
Parmesan cheese	1 tablespoon melted
¼ teaspoon salt	butter

Preheat oven to 400 degrees F.
Break eggs and slip into a buttered shallow baking pan. Sprinkle with cheese, salt and ham. Drizzle butter over eggs. Bake until eggs are set. Serve immediately.

POACHED EGGS WITH CREAM SAUCE

(Makes 4 servings)

½ cup light cream	4 slices allowed bread,
Salt to taste	toasted
4 eggs	¼ cup Cheddar cheese

Heat cream to the boiling point in a frying pan. Add salt. Lower heat. Break each egg separately into a saucer. Slip each egg carefully into heated cream. Spoon cream over eggs. Cook until eggs are set. Place each egg on a slice of hot toast. Add cheese to cream and cook until cheese melts, stirring frequently. Spoon hot sauce over each egg. Serve immediately.

FRIED EGGS AND GRATED CHEESE

(Makes 2 servings)

4 tablespoons butter
4 eggs
Salt to taste

Pepper to taste
1 tablespoon grated
Parmesan cheese

Preheat oven to 450 degrees F.

In a large, heavy skillet, melt butter. Carefully slip eggs into pan. Cook until eggs are almost set. Sprinkle salt, pepper and cheese over eggs. Place under hot broiler until cheese melts. Serve immediately.

CHEESE AND MUSHROOM QUICHE

(Makes 8 servings)

Plain pastry (recipe
page 161)
2 tablespoons butter
1¼ cups thinly sliced
mushrooms
2 slices bacon,
cooked, drained
and crumbled

1 cup Swiss cheese,
cubed
1 onion, minced
4 eggs, lightly beaten
2 cups heavy cream
½ teaspoon nutmeg
½ teaspoon pepper

Preheat oven to 400 degrees F.

Line a 9-inch pie plate with pastry. Refrigerate. In a saucepan, melt butter. Add mushrooms and sauté for 3 minutes. In a bowl, combine mushrooms, bacon, cheese and onion. Sprinkle over prepared pie plate. Combine eggs, cream, nutmeg and pepper. Pour over cheese mixture. Bake for 10 minutes. Reduce heat to 300 degrees F. and bake 20 minutes more. Serve hot or cold.

STUFFED EGGS SUPREME

6 hard-cooked eggs
1 can (7½ ounces) crabmeat, drained and flaked
¼ cup finely chopped celery
1 tablespoon lemon juice
¼ cup finely chopped green onions
1 tablespoon chopped parsley
½ cup mayonnaise
½ teaspoon salt

Cut eggs in half, lengthwise, and remove yolks. Set egg whites aside. In a bowl, mash egg yolks. Add crabmeat, celery, lemon juice, onion, parsley, mayonnaise and salt. Mix well. Chill. At serving time, stuff egg whites with crabmeat mixture. Arrange on a serving plate. May be served as a salad, appetizers or hors d'oeuvres.

EGG AND CHEESE PANCAKES

(Makes 4 servings)

2 tablespoons salad oil
4 eggs, lightly beaten
2 tablespoons finely chopped onion
½ cup oat flour
1 teaspoon baking powder
½ teaspoon salt
⅛ teaspoon pepper
1½ cups shredded Cheddar cheese
Butter

In a bowl, combine salad oil, eggs, onion, oat flour, baking powder, salt and pepper. Mix well. Stir in cheese. Heat butter on a hot griddle. Pour ⅓ cup of mixture onto griddle for each pancake. Cook until well browned on each side. Serve immediately.

HAM AND CHEESE FILLING
FOR PINWHEELS

Prepare batter for "The Bread" (page 27)
2 tablespoons finely chopped onion
1 teaspoon prepared mustard
2 tablespoons chopped green pepper
½ pound sharp Cheddar cheese, grated
¼ pound boiled ham, finely chopped
5 tablespoons melted butter

Preheat oven to 350 degrees F.

Oil a jelly-roll pan. Line it with waxed paper. Oil the paper and spoon the prepared batter into the prepared pan. Bake for 12–15 minutes. Invert the pan onto a towel. Remove pan and peel off paper. Roll towel and bread. Cool. In a bowl, combine onion, mustard, green pepper, Cheddar cheese, ham, and melted butter. Spread mixture evenly over roll. Roll up again. Bake until the cheese melts. Cut roll into slices and serve immediately.

ITALIAN EGG PIE

(Makes 6 servings)

Plain pastry (see recipe page 161)
6 eggs
¼ cup milk
1 can (7 ounces) tuna fish, drained and flaked
½ pound Mozzarella cheese, grated
¼ teaspoon salt
¼ teaspoon pepper
½ teaspoon basil
½ teaspoon oregano

Preheat oven to 425 degrees F.

Line a 9-inch pie plate with pastry. Trim edge and flute. In a bowl, combine eggs and milk. Mix well. Add remaining ingredients. Blend thoroughly. Pour into prepared pie plate. Bake for 20 minutes. Lower oven heat to 350, and bake 15–20 minutes longer. Serve hot.

RICOTTA PIZZA

Plain pastry (see recipe page 161)
1½ pounds Ricotta cheese, sieved
¼ teaspoon salt
⅛ teaspoon pepper
2 eggs, well beaten
¼ pound Prosciutto ham, chopped

Preheat oven to 375 degrees F.

Line bottom of a shallow baking dish with pastry. Chill. In a bowl, combine cheese, salt, pepper, eggs and ham. Mix thoroughly. Spoon mixture over prepared pan. Bake for 50 minutes. Cool and serve in slices.

CHEDDAR CHEESE BALLS

(Makes about 40)

1 pound grated Cheddar cheese
¾ cup chopped ripe olives
5 tablespoons soft butter
Few drops Tabasco
½ clove garlic, finely chopped
Few grains cayenne pepper

In a bowl, combine all ingredients. Form mixture into walnut-size balls. Chill. To serve put a cocktail pick into each ball.

MACARONI AND CHEESE

(Makes 6 servings)

1 tablespoon butter
1 cup milk
Salt to taste
Pepper to taste
½ pound Cheddar
   cheese, shredded

2½ cups cooked
   Jerusalem artichoke
   macaroni
Toasted soybeans,
   coarsely crushed

Preheat oven to 350 degrees F.

In a saucepan, melt butter. Add milk, salt and pepper. Mix well. Remove from heat. Add cheese and stir until melted. Combine sauce and macaroni. Pour into a buttered casserole. Sprinkle top of casserole generously with soybeans. Bake for 25 minutes. Serve hot.

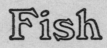

Fish

ALMOND TOMATO FILLETS

(Makes 3–4 servings)

¼ cup oat flour
½ teaspoon salt
¼ teaspoon pepper
1 pound flounder
  fillets
¼ cup salad oil
1 tablespoon
  margarine

4 cups chopped
  tomatoes, peeled
½ clove garlic, minced
½ teaspoon salt
½ teaspoon tarragon
¼ cup blanched
  almonds, slivered
  and toasted

Combine oat flour, salt and ⅛ teaspoon pepper. Coat fillets with oat flour mixture. Heat salad oil in a heavy skillet. Fry fillets over low heat until golden brown, 2–3 minutes. Turn and brown on other side. In another skillet, melt margarine. Add tomatoes, garlic, salt, tarragon and remaining pepper. Cover and cook over low heat about 3 minutes. To serve, arrange tomatoes on a platter. Top with fillets. Garnish with almonds.

ARLENE'S SALMON MOUSSE

(Makes 4–6 servings)

1 envelope unflavored gelatin	¼ teaspoon paprika
2 tablespoons lemon juice	1 teaspoon dried dill weed
1 onion, sliced	1 can (1 pound) salmon, drained
½ cup boiling water	1 cup heavy cream
½ cup mayonnaise	

Put gelatin, lemon juice, onion and water into a blender container. Blend 1 minute at high speed. Add mayonnaise, paprika, dill weed and salmon. Blend 1 minute at high speed. Add cream, ⅓ cup at a time, blending ½ minute after each addition. Pour into a 4-cup mold. Chill until firm. Unmold.

BAKED FISH AND CHEESE

(Makes 3–4 servings)

1 pound fish fillets	2 medium onions, chopped
6 slices American cheese	2 tablespoons oat flour
¼ cup chopped parsley	⅛ teaspoon salt
1 teaspoon oregano	⅛ teaspoon pepper
¼ cup salad oil	1½ cups milk

Preheat oven to 400 degrees F.

In a buttered, oblong baking dish, alternate layers of fish and cheese, ending with cheese. Sprinkle with parsley and oregano. Set aside. Heat salad oil in a heavy skillet. Add onions and cook until tender. Stir in oat flour, salt and pepper. Add milk. Cook, stirring constantly, until mixture thickens. Pour over fish. Bake for 25–30 minutes, or until fish flakes easily with a fork.

OAT-CRUSTED FISH FILLETS

(Makes 3 servings)

6 fish fillets
Salt to taste
Pepper to taste

Oatmeal
½ cup butter

Sprinkle fillets with salt and pepper. Coat with oatmeal. Melt butter in a heavy skillet. Add fillets and sauté until lightly browned on both sides.

SHRIMP ITALIAN

(Makes 4 servings)

⅓ cup salad oil
1 pound shrimp, shelled and deveined
2 tablespoons chopped celery
½ tablespoon chopped green pepper
1 tablespoon chopped onion

1 clove garlic, minced
1 tablespoon chopped parsley
⅓ cup water
2 tablespoons lemon juice
⅓ cup tomato paste
½ teaspoon salt
⅛ teaspoon celery salt

Heat oil in a heavy skillet. Add shrimp, celery, green pepper, onion and garlic. Sauté over medium heat, turning often, until shrimp turn pink. Reduce heat. Add remaining ingredients. Mix well. Simmer, stirring occasionally, for about 5 minutes, or until thoroughly heated.

SCALLOPS CACCIATORE

(Makes 4 servings)

¼ cup salad oil
1 pound sea scallops, cut into halves
1 medium onion, chopped
1 medium green pepper, chopped
1 clove garlic, minced
1 can (1 pound) tomatoes, drained
1 can (8 ounces) tomato sauce
1¼ teaspoon salt
⅛ teaspoon pepper
2 bay leaves
2 tablespoons chopped parsley

Heat oil in a heavy skillet. Add scallops. Cook over medium (turning once) heat until tender, about 5 minutes. Remove from skillet with a slotted spoon. In same skillet, combine onion, green pepper and garlic. Cook over low heat for about 3 minutes, or until tender. Add scallops, tomatoes, tomato sauce, salt, pepper and bay leaves. Heat thoroughly. Serve immediately, garnished with parsley.

SHRIMP PIQUANT

(Makes 4 servings)

¼ cup salad oil
½ cup cider vinegar
Few drops liquid non-caloric liquid sweetener
¼ cup finely chopped onion
¼ cup finely chopped green pepper
¼ cup finely chopped, cooked green beans
1 tablespoon finely chopped pimento
¼ cup finely chopped cucumber
24 large shrimp, cooked and chilled
Crisp greens

In a bowl, combine salad oil, vinegar and liquid sweetener. Add remaining ingredients, except shrimp and greens. Blend well. Refrigerate for several hours. Add shrimp. Serve on a bed of crisp greens.

Sauces for Fish

LEMON-PARSLEY SAUCE

(Makes about ½ cup)

½ cup margarine, melted

1 teaspoon grated lemon rind

3 tablespoons lemon juice

1 tablespoon chopped parsley

Combine all ingredients in a saucepan. Heat thoroughly. Serve hot over broiled or baked fish.

SAVORY SAUCE

(Makes 1⅓ cups)

1 cup margarine

⅓ cup finely chopped celery

3 tablespoons finely chopped parsley

2 tablespoons finely chopped onion

1 clove garlic, minced

Salt to taste

Pepper to taste

Melt margarine in saucepan. Add remaining ingredients. Cook until celery is tender. Serve hot over baked or broiled fish.

CREOLE SAUCE

(Makes about 2 cups)

2 tablespoons
margarine
¼ cup minced onion
¼ cup chopped
pimento-stuffed
green olives
⅓ cup chopped green
pepper

1½ cups finely chopped
tomatoes
¼ teaspoon salt
Few drops noncaloric
liquid sweetener
Dash cayenne pepper

Melt margarine in a heavy skillet. Add onion, olives and green pepper. Sauté until onion is lightly browned. Add remaining ingredients. Simmer 10–15 minutes. Serve hot over broiled or baked fish.

Main Dishes

Chicken

BARBECUED CHICKEN

(Makes 6 servings)

3 broiler chickens, split   Melted butter

Barbecue Sauce

1½ tablespoons tomato
   paste
Few drops Tabasco
   sauce
½ teaspoon paprika
¼ teaspoon dry
   mustard
1 teaspoon salt

1 clove garlic, mashed
⅓ cup salad oil
1 teaspoon grated
   onion
½ cup cider vinegar
¼ teaspoon ground
   ginger

Brush chicken with butter and place on a broiler rack about 4 inches from heat. Broil 10 minutes on each side. Combine sauce ingredients in a bowl. Brush chicken with sauce and broil 20 minutes longer, turning and basting frequently.

BREAST OF CHICKEN PROVENCALE

(Makes 4 servings)

2 chicken breasts
Paprika
1½ teaspoons salt
1 teaspoon dried
   tarragon
2 green peppers,
   sliced

2 tomatoes, peeled
   and quartered
1 medium onion,
   sliced
½ cup chicken stock

Preheat oven to 500 degrees F.

Remove skin from chicken and cut breasts in half.
Place breasts in a shallow baking pan. Sprinkle both
sides with paprika, salt, and tarragon. Broil chicken
just until browned, turning once. Reduce oven to 350
degrees F. Transfer chicken to a shallow baking dish.
Add vegetables and stock. Bake for 20 minutes, or until chicken and vegetables are tender.

CHICKEN AND CHEESE SOUFFLE

(Makes 6 servings)

4 tablespoons butter
4 tablespoons oat
   flour
1 teaspoon salt
⅛ teaspoon pepper
1½ cups milk

4 eggs, separated
1 cup shredded
   Cheddar cheese
2 cups chicken,
   cooked and finely
   chopped

Preheat oven to 325 degrees F.

Melt butter in a saucepan. Add flour, salt and pepper. Cook over low heat, stirring until well blended. Add milk and stir until mixture begins to thicken. In a bowl, beat egg yolks well. Gradually add egg yolks to the mixture. Add cheese and chicken. Mix well. Beat egg whites until stiff. Fold into mixture. Pour into ungreased soufflé dish. Bake for 50 minutes. Serve immediately.

CHICKEN CACCIATORE

(Makes 4 servings)

¼ cup salad oil	1 teaspoon salt
1 3-pound chicken cut up	¼ teaspoon pepper
1 clove garlic, minced	1 bay leaf
2 onions, chopped	½ teaspoon basil
1 can (1 pound) Italian tomatoes	1 teaspoon oregano
1 can (8 ounces) tomato sauce	Grated Parmesan cheese

Heat oil in a large skillet. Add chicken, garlic and onions. Cook until lightly browned, turning once. Add tomatoes, tomato sauce, salt, pepper, bay leaf, basil and oregano. Cover and simmer for 50 minutes, or until chicken is tender. Spoon off excess fat and remove bay leaf. To serve, place chicken on a platter and sprinkle with grated cheese. Serve immediately.

CHICKEN IN LEMON SAUCE

(Makes 4 servings)

1 3½-pound chicken, cut into serving pieces
2½ cups water
2 bay leaves
2 teaspoons salt
12 small white onions, peeled

1 package (9 ounces) frozen artichoke hearts
2 tablespoons oat flour
2 egg yolks
2 tablespoons lemon juice

Put chicken, 2 cups water, bay leaves and salt in a large, heavy pot. Bring to boil. Cover pot, reduce heat and simmer for 25 minutes. Add onions and simmer for 15 minutes. Add artichoke hearts and simmer for 10 minutes more. Combine the remaining ½ cup of water, oat flour, egg yolks and lemon juice in a bowl. Blend until smooth. Gradually add to chicken, stirring constantly. Cook until sauce is slightly thickened.

PINEAPPLE CHICKEN

(Makes 3–4 servings)

1 3½-pound chicken, cut into eighths
1 teaspoon paprika
1½ teaspoons salt
⅛ teaspoon pepper
¼ cup butter

½ cup orange juice
1 cup crushed, unsweetened pineapple
1 orange, peeled and sliced

Preheat oven to 350 degrees F.

Sprinkle the chicken with paprika, salt and pepper. Melt butter in a large ovenproof casserole. Add chicken and cook until browned on all sides. Pour orange juice over chicken and top with pineapple. Cover and bake until the chicken is tender. Arrange orange slices on top of chicken and bake uncovered for 10 minutes longer.

CHICKEN MOROCCO

(Makes 4 servings)

1 3½-pound chicken, cut into serving pieces	1 clove garlic, stuck with a food pick
Paprika	1 medium eggplant, peeled and diced
2 teaspoons salt	4 scallions, chopped
¼ teaspoon ground pepper	2 tomatoes, peeled and diced
2 tablespoons butter	¼ teaspoon thyme
½ cup chicken stock	1 tablespoon chopped parsley

Sprinkle chicken pieces with paprika, 1 teaspoon salt and pepper. Melt butter in a heavy skillet. Add chicken pieces, skin side down, and cook until lightly browned. Remove from skillet. Add stock, scraping brown particles from bottom of the skillet. Add garlic, eggplant, scallions and tomatoes. Sprinkle with remaining salt, thyme and parsley. Cover and simmer 30 minutes. Remove garlic and serve.

CHICKEN STEW

(Makes 6 servings)

2 tablespoons salad oil
1 onion, chopped
1 3½-pound chicken, cut into serving pieces
12 mushrooms, sliced
3 carrots, sliced
1 green pepper, sliced
1 tomato, chopped
1 cup water
Salt to taste
Pepper to taste
1 tablespoon paprika
½ cup sour cream

In a large heavy skillet, heat oil. Add onion and cook until golden brown. Add chicken and brown on all sides. Add mushrooms, carrots, green pepper, tomato, water, salt, pepper and paprika. Cover and cook over low heat until chicken is tender, about 40 minutes. Stir in sour cream and serve.

CHICKEN CLEOPATRA

(Makes 4 servings)

1 3½-pound chicken, cut into serving pieces
1 teaspoon salt
1 teaspoon paprika
¼ teaspoon pepper
2 tablespoons salad oil
1 cup water
¼ teaspoon turmeric
⅛ teaspoon ground cardamon
½ teaspoon curry powder
⅛ teaspoon dry mustard
1 medium onion, sliced
1 tablespoon oat flour

Sprinkle chicken with salt, paprika and pepper. Heat oil in a heavy skillet. Place chicken, skin side down, in hot oil. Brown on both sides. Add ¾ cup water, spices and onion. Cover skillet and cook 30 minutes, or until chicken is tender. Remove chicken to warm serving platter. Blend oat flour with remaining ¼ cup of water. Quickly add to pan drippings in skillet, stirring constantly. Reduce heat and cook sauce for 2 minutes more. To serve, pour hot sauce over chicken.

CHICKEN LITTLE

(Makes 4 servings)

1 3½-pound chicken, cut into serving pieces	¼ teaspoon savory
	¼ teaspoon thyme
	1 clove garlic, minced
1 teaspoon salt	1 medium onion, minced
⅛ teaspoon pepper	
½ teaspoon paprika	1 medium green pepper, cut into strips
2 tablespoons salad oil	
Juice of ½ lemon	½ pound mushrooms, sliced
½ cup water	

Sprinkle chicken with salt, pepper and paprika. Heat oil in a heavy skillet. Place chicken, skin side down, in hot oil. Brown 20 minutes on both sides. Add lemon juice, water, herbs and garlic. Cover skillet and cook over medium heat for 10 minutes. Add vegetables. Cover and cook for 10 minutes longer, or until chicken and vegetables are tender.

Beef

BEEF-VEGETABLE SOUP STEW

(Makes 6–8 servings)

1 tablespoon salad oil
1½ pounds lean stewing
beef, cut into 1-inch
cubes
1 cup sliced onion
4 cups water
2 tablespoons beef
seasoning
3 teaspoons salt
6 whole peppercorns

1 bay leaf
1 can (1 pound)
tomatoes
1 can (1 pound)
green beans,
drained
2 cups carrots, sliced
5 cups cabbage,
coarsely shredded

Heat oil in a Dutch oven. Add meat and brown evenly on all sides. Add onion and cook until tender. Add 2 cups water, beef seasoning, 2 teaspoons salt, peppercorns and bay leaf. Cover and simmer for 1½ hours.

Add tomatoes, green beans and carrots. Cover and simmer until carrots are tender, about ½ hour. Add remaining water, remaining salt and cabbage. Cover and simmer until cabbage is just tender, about 10 minutes.

ALOHA BURGERS

(Makes 8 servings)

1 can (1 pound, 4 ounces) sliced, unsweetened pineapple
⅔ cup soy sauce
1 teaspoon ground ginger
2 cloves garlic, thinly sliced
2 pounds lean ground beef

⅔ cup thinly sliced green onion
½ cup crushed toasted soy beans
2 eggs
½ teaspoon salt
⅛ teaspoon pepper
½ cup chopped Macadamia nuts
1 tablespoon butter, melted

Preheat broiler to 475 degrees F.

Drain pineapple and reserve 1 cup juice. Combine juice, soy sauce, ginger and garlic in a bowl. Set aside. In another bowl, combine beef, onion, soy beans, eggs, salt, pepper and ½ cup of the juice and soy sauce mixture. Mix well. Shape meat into 8 4-inch patties. Place patties in a shallow pan and spoon remaining juice and soy sauce mixture over the meat. Cover and refrigerate for 1 hour, turning patties once. Drain patties and broil 3–4 inches from heat, for 12–14 minutes, turning once. Broil pineapple slices during last 2–3 minutes of cooking time. Brown nuts lightly in melted butter. To serve, place pineapple slices on a serving platter. Top each slice with a burger. Spoon nuts over all.

CHILI CON CARNE

(Makes 6 servings)

3 tablespoons salad oil
1 onion, sliced
1 pound lean ground beef
1 clove garlic
2 cups soybeans, cooked or canned

2½ cups canned tomatoes
1 tablespoon chili powder
Salt to taste
Pepper to taste

Heat the oil in a heavy skillet. Add onion and cook two minutes. Add beef and garlic. Cook, breaking up meat with a fork, over low heat for 10 minutes. Add soybeans, tomatoes, chili powder, salt and pepper. Cover skillet and simmer until sauce is thick.

SPICY BEEF ROAST

(Makes 10–12 servings)

5 pounds lean chuck roast
½ bay leaf
2 teaspoons salt
1 teaspoon pepper
2 onions, sliced
½ teaspoon ground ginger
1 teaspoon cinnamon
Cider vinegar

2 cups water
2 tablespoons butter
2 parsnips, ground
1 medium rutabaga, ground
4 carrots, ground
2 onions, ground
3 ribs celery, ground
Salt to taste

Preheat oven to 325 degrees F.
Place meat in a large bowl. Add bay leaf, 2 tea-

spoons salt, pepper, sliced onions, ginger, cinnamon and enough vinegar to cover meat. Refrigerate for at least 12 hours. Drain meat, reserving marinade, and place in a roasting pan. In a saucepan, combine ½ of the marinade and water. Bring to a boil. Pour over the meat and roast for 3 hours. In a large skillet, melt butter. Add ground vegetables and salt. Sauté for 4 minutes. Pour vegetables over roast after 2 hours. Continue cooking until roast is done.

HEARTY BEEF STEW

(Makes 6 servings)

4 strips bacon, cut into 1-inch strips
2 tablespoons margarine
1 pound boneless lean chuck, cut into 1-inch cubes
2 cups chopped onion
2 cups peeled, chopped cooking apples

1 cup beef broth
2 cups water
1½ teaspoons salt
2 cups sliced carrots
1 pound smoked ham, cut into 1½-inch strips
4 cups cabbage, coarsely shredded

In a heavy Dutch oven, fry bacon over moderate heat until crisp. Drain on paper toweling and set aside. To bacon drippings in pot, add margarine and beef. Brown meat evenly on all sides. Add onion and apple. Cook until apple is tender. Add broth, water and salt. Cover pot and simmer until meat is tender, about 2 hours. Thirty minutes before end of cooking time, add carrots and ham. Ten minutes before end of cooking time, add cabbage and reserved bacon. Simmer gently until cabbage is tender.

ITALIAN MEATLOAF

(Makes 8 servings)

2 pounds lean ground
   beef
2 eggs
¼ cup quick-cooking
   oatmeal
½ cup finely chopped
   onion
1 clove garlic, minced
1 tablespoon chopped
   parsley

2 teaspoons salt
1 teaspoon basil
¼ teaspoon pepper
½ cup tomato juice
4 squares sliced
   Mozzarella cheese,
   cut in half
   diagonally

Preheat oven to 350 degrees F.

In a large bowl, combine all ingredients, except cheese. Mix well. Shape into a round loaf about 7 inches in diameter. Place in a lightly oiled shallow pan. Bake about 1 hour 15 minutes, or until done. Arrange cheese slices on top in a spiral, with ends overlapping at center top. Return to oven. Heat just until cheese melts. Cut in wedges to serve.

SAVORY MEAT PATTIES

(Makes 3–4 servings)

½ pound lean ground
   beef
½ pound ground veal
1½ teaspoons salt
⅛ teaspoon pepper
½ teaspoon celery salt

½ teaspoon paprika
1 egg, well beaten
¼ teaspoon minced
   onion
½ pound mushrooms,
   sautéed

Preheat broiler to 450 degrees F.

In a bowl combine all ingredients, except mushrooms. Shape meat into patties. Broil 4–6 inches from heat, turning once, until meat reaches desired degree of doneness. Serve with sautéed mushrooms.

ARLENE'S BEEF ROULADE

(Makes 4 servings)

2 tablespoons butter	1 teaspoon parsley, chopped
¾ pound lean ground beef	1 teaspoon oregano
1 medium onion, chopped	1 teaspoon rosemary
1 can (4 ounces) mushrooms, stems and pieces, drained	1 bay leaf, crumbled
½ teaspoon salt	2 cups coarsely crumbled sharp Cheddar cheese
Dash pepper	1 cup grated Parmesan cheese
1 teaspoon dry mustard	8 7-inch crêpes
2 cloves garlic, minced	16 thin slices Mozzarella cheese
½ cup catsup	Paprika
	Melted butter

Preheat oven to 400 degrees F.

In a large skillet, melt butter. Add beef, onions and mushrooms. Cook over medium heat, breaking up meat with a fork, until browned. Add salt, pepper, mustard and garlic. Simmer for 5 minutes. Add catsup, herbs, Cheddar cheese and ½ cup Parmesan cheese. Cover and simmer until cheese is half-melted. Remove from heat. Spread mixture on crêpes. Roll up crêpes and place in a greased baking dish, seam side down. Sprinkle with remaining Parmesan cheese. Place 2 slices of Mozzarella cheese on each roll. Sprinkle with paprika and drizzle with melted butter. Bake 15 minutes, or until thoroughly heated and Mozzarella cheese is melted.

HAMBURGER PARMIGIANA

(Makes 6 servings)

2 pounds lean ground beef

2 cups tomato sauce, heated

2 tablespoons grated Parmesan cheese

6 slices Mozzarella cheese

Preheat broiler to 450 degrees F.

Shape beef into 6 patties. Broil 5 minutes on each side. Remove from broiler. Arrange patties in a shallow ovenproof dish. Spoon hot sauce evenly over patties. Sprinkle with Parmesan cheese. Top each pattie with a slice of Mozzarella cheese. Broil under moderate heat until cheese melts. Serve immediately.

SPAGHETTI SAUCE WITH MEATBALLS

(Makes about 2 quarts)

1 pound lean ground beef

1 onion, chopped

1 slice bread (allowed), soaked in water

2 eggs, slightly beaten

½ teaspoon salt

¼ teaspoon pepper

½ cup salad oil

1 clove garlic, minced

1 can (28 ounces) tomato puree

2 cups cold water

1 cup chopped celery

In a bowl, combine beef, onion, bread, eggs, salt and pepper. Mix thoroughly. Shape into 1½-inch balls. Heat oil in a heavy skillet. Add garlic. Cook for 1 minute. Add meatballs and brown on all sides. Add tomato puree, water and celery. Simmer over low heat until sauce is thickened.

Lamb

BRAISED LAMB WITH VEGETABLES

(Makes 6–8 servings)

¼ cup salad oil
1 shoulder of lamb, boned and rolled
1 large onion, sliced
½ cup diced turnip
1 clove garlic, chopped
½ cup diced carrots

¾ cup diced celery
1 can (1 pound) tomatoes
2 cups boiling water
2 teaspoons salt
¼ teaspoon pepper
½ bay leaf

Heat oil in a large, heavy saucepan. Add lamb and brown quickly on all sides. Remove the meat. Add onion, turnip, garlic, carrots and celery. Cook for 10 minutes, stirring frequently. Return meat to pan. Add tomatoes, water, salt, pepper and bay leaf. Cover pan and simmer for about 2 hours, or until the meat is tender. To serve, slice meat and arrange on a heated platter. Spoon vegetable sauce over meat.

PEPPERY BARBECUED LEG OF LAMB

(Makes 6–8 servings)

1 leg of lamb (6–7 pounds)	Salt
	Oregano
Lemon juice	Crushed red pepper

Brush meat on all sides with lemon juice. Sprinkle all sides with salt and oregano. Generously sprinkle all sides with red pepper, taking care to press pepper into the fat side of the meat. Skewer lamb with rotisserie spit. Insert meat thermometer into heaviest part of the leg. Place spit about 8 inches above gray hot coals. Roast 30 minutes per pound or until meat thermometer registers desired degree of doneness.

BARBECUED LAMB RIBLETS

(Makes 6 servings)

5 pounds lamb riblets	½ cup unsweetened pineapple juice
Salt to taste	
Pepper to taste	1½ teaspoons non-
¾ cup catsup	caloric liquid sweetener

Preheat broiler to 475 degrees F.

Parboil lamb riblets in a large pot of boiling salted water until tender, about 45 minutes. Drain well. Trim off excess fat and sprinkle lamb lightly with salt and pepper. Combine catsup, pineapple juice and liquid sweetener in a saucepan. Simmer about 5 minutes. Brush riblets on both sides with the sauce. Broil riblets until browned on both sides, brushing frequently with sauce.

HERB-MUSTARD GLAZED LEG OF LAMB

(Makes 6–8 servings)

1 leg of lamb (6–7 pounds)	1 teaspoon rosemary
½ cup spicy brown prepared mustard	2 tablespoons salad oil
1 clove garlic	3 tablespoons water

Preheat oven to 325 degrees F.

Place lamb on rack in a shallow roasting pan. Roast for 30–35 minutes per pound, or until meat thermometer registers 175 degrees, or desired degree of doneness. In a bowl combine remaining ingredients and baste meat frequently during the last 1½ hours of roasting time.

CURRY BROILED LOIN LAMB CHOPS

(Makes 4 servings)

1 tablespoon butter	½ teaspoon dried *fines herbes*
1 teaspoon curry powder	¼ cup bouillon
Few drops noncaloric liquid sweetener	4 loin chops, about ¾ inch thick

Preheat broiler to 500 degrees F.

In a medium saucepan, melt butter. Add curry powder, liquid sweetener, *herbes* and bouillon. Mix well. Cook over low heat, stirring occasionally for 3–4 minutes. Brush lamb with half of curry mixture. Broil the chops 3–4 inches from heat for 5–7 minutes. Turn chops, and brush with remaining curry mixture. Broil 5–7 minutes or until desired degree of doneness.

PAN-FRIED RIB LAMB CHOPS
WITH MUSHROOMS

(Makes 6 servings)

6 rib lamb chops
Salt to taste
Pepper to taste
4 tablespoons butter
1 clove garlic, halved

1 can (4 ounces)
button mushrooms,
drained
¼ teaspoon dried
fines herbes
1 teaspoon lemon
juice

Sprinkle chops with salt and pepper. Melt 2 tablespoons butter in a heavy skillet. Add chops and garlic. Cook over medium heat for about 12 minutes, turning once, or until chops are browned on both sides. Discard garlic. Remove chops to a serving plate and keep warm. Add remaining butter, mushrooms, *fines herbes* and lemon juice to pan. Sauté until mushrooms are lightly browned. Pour mushroom butter sauce over the chops and serve immediately.

LEG OF LAMB WITH ONION SAUCE

(Makes 6–8 servings)

1 leg of lamb (6–7
pounds)
Salt to taste
Pepper to taste
2 tablespoons salad
oil
1 cup chopped onion

1 clove garlic,
crushed
1 cup beef bouillon
1 tablespoon vinegar
2 tablespoons
chopped parsley
⅛ teaspoon cayenne
pepper

Preheat oven to 325 degrees F.

Sprinkle lamb with salt and pepper. Place on a rack in a shallow roasting pan. Roast for 30–35 minutes per pound, or until meat thermometer registers desired degree of doneness. Heat salad oil in a large skillet. Add onion and garlic. Sauté for 2–3 minutes. Add bouillon, vinegar, parsley and cayenne pepper. Heat thoroughly. About 45 minutes before the lamb is done, drain off drippings. Pour onion sauce over lamb and continue roasting, basting frequently, until lamb is done.

ROAST SHOULDER OF LAMB

(Makes 10 servings)

¼ pound salt pork	1½ teaspoons salt
1 medium onion, chopped	⅛ teaspoon pepper
¼ teaspoon basil	1 5-pound shoulder of lamb, boned
¼ teaspoon ground sage	Salt
3 tablespoons chopped parsley	Pepper

Preheat oven to 300 degrees F.

Cook salt pork in a heavy skillet until golden in color. Remove pork and discard. Drain off all but 1½ tablespoons of the fat. Add onion and cook until tender. Add basil, sage, parsley, 1½ teaspoons salt and ⅛ teaspoon pepper. Cook for 1 minute. Place lamb on a flat surface. Spread cooked mixture evenly over meat. Roll up meat and tie in several places with heavy thread. Place on a rack in a roasting pan, fat side up. Sprnkle with additional salt and pepper. Roast for about 3½ hours or until meat is tender.

BROILED LOIN LAMB CHOPS

(Makes 4 servings)

¼ cup salad oil
3 tablespoons lemon juice
⅓ cup chopped pimento-stuffed olives
1 clove garlic, crushed

½ teaspoon salt
¼ teaspoon oregano
¼ teaspoon basil
⅛ teaspoon pepper
4 loin lamb chops, 1 inch thick

In a bowl, combine oil, lemon juice, olives and seasonings. Place chops in a shallow dish. Pour marinade over chops. Chill for 2–3 hours, turning chops once. Preheat oven to 500 degrees F. Drain chops, reserving marinade. Broil 3–4 inches from heat for 8 minutes on each side. Heat reserved marinade in a small saucepan and pour over chops before serving.

TANGY LAMB AND VEGETABLES EN BROCHETTE

(Makes 6 servings)

½ cup catsup
½ cup salad oil
½ cup water
1 tablespoon prepared mustard
1½ pounds boneless lean lamb, cut into 1½-inch cubes

½ pound large mushrooms
2 ribs celery, cut into ½-inch slices, parboiled
2 medium red onions, cut into sixths

Combine catsup, salad oil, water and mustard in a large bowl. Add lamb. Marinate several hours in refrigerator, turning meat occasionally. Drain lamb, reserving marinade. Preheat broiler to 475 degrees F. Place lamb and vegetables on separate skewers. Broil lamb 5–6 inches from heat for 15 minutes, turning once and brushing frequently with marinade. After 3 minutes, place vegetables in broiler. Broil 12 minutes, turning once, brushing frequently with marinade. Remove meat and vegetables. Serve immediately.

FRICASSEE OF LAMB WITH VEGETABLES

(Makes 6–8 servings)

½ cup salad oil
2 pounds boneless lamb, cut into 1½-inch cubes
2 cups boiling water
¼ cup chopped onion
5 sprigs parsley
1 bay leaf
8 peppercorns
4 whole cloves
2 teaspoons salt
¾ cup sliced green beans
¾ cup sliced celery
¾ cup diced turnip
½ cup diced parsnip
6 small white onions
½ cup diced carrots

Heat oil in a large, heavy saucepan. Add meat and brown on all sides. Add water, chopped onion, parsley, bay leaf, peppercorns, cloves and salt. Cover pan and reduce heat. Simmer for 1½ hours. Add vegetables and cook for 30 minutes longer, or until the meat and vegetables are tender. Remove from heat. Spoon 1 cup vegetables into a blender container. Blend until smooth. Stir puree into lamb mixture. Return to range and heat thoroughly.

BROILED LOIN LAMB CHOPS PARMESAN

(Makes 4 servings)

4 loin lamb chops,
   1 inch thick
Onion salt to taste
Pepper to taste

3 tablespoons grated
   Parmesan cheese
¼ teaspoon garlic
   powder
¼ teaspoon oregano

Preheat broiler to 500 degrees F.

Sprinkle both sides of lamb with onion salt and pepper. Broil 3–4 inches from heat for 7 minutes. Turn and broil 8 minutes longer. Combine Parmesan cheese, garlic powder and oregano. Sprinkle over lamb. Broil lamb 2 minutes longer, or until it reaches the desired degree of doneness.

LAMB AND VEGETABLES

(Makes 4 servings)

1 tablespoon salad oil
2 pounds boned
   stewing lamb, cut
   into 1-inch cubes
Salt to taste
¼ teaspoon pepper
2 bay leaves

2 cups cold water
1 medium cabbage,
   quartered
2 carrots, quartered
2 parsnips, quartered
½ tablespoon dill weed

Heat oil in a large skillet. Add meat and brown on all sides. Add salt, pepper, bay leaves and water. Bring to a boil. Cover skillet and simmer for 15 minutes. Add cabbage, carrots, parsnips and dill weed. Cook over medium heat for 30 minutes, or until meat and vegetables are tender. Remove bay leaves.

Pork

PORK STUFFING FOR FOWL

(Makes about 5 cups)

2½ pounds lean pork, finely ground
¼ cup chopped parsley
1 clove garlic, minced
1 teaspoon thyme
1 teaspoon salt
2 eggs, slightly beaten

1 teaspoon pepper
¼ teaspoon nutmeg
1 teaspoon sage
½ teaspoon chopped chives
½ teaspoon Tabasco

Brown pork in a large, heavy skillet, breaking up meat with a fork. Remove from heat and add remaining ingredients. Mix well. Refrigerate until ready to use.

SAUSAGE MEAT PATTIES

(Makes 3–4 servings)

1 pound lean pork, ground
1 teaspoon salt

½ teaspoon pepper
½ teaspoon sage
¼ teaspoon thyme

Preheat broiler to 450 degrees F.
In a large bowl combine all ingredients. Mix well. Shape into 4 patties. Broil for about 10 minutes on each side.

SPARERIBS WITH SAUERKRAUT

(Makes 4–6 servings)

3 pounds spareribs, cut into serving pieces	2 cups tomato juice
1½ teaspoons salt	2 carrots, shredded
¼ teaspoon pepper	½ cup finely chopped onion
2 apples, peeled and chopped	1 tablespoon dill seed
	1½ pounds sauerkraut

Preheat oven to 350 degrees F.

Sprinkle spareribs with salt and pepper. Place meat in a heavy skillet. Combine remaining ingredients and spoon over ribs. Cover skillet and bake for 2½–3 hours, or until ribs are done. Baste ribs several times during last hour with pan juices.

Veal

CRUSTED VEAL CUTLETS

Oat flour
Italian-style veal cutlets

Slightly beaten egg
Butter or salad oil

Dip cutlets in oat flour, coating both sides. Dip in egg and then in flour again. Set aside in refrigerator until ready to use. Heat butter or oil in a heavy skillet. Add cutlets, one at a time. Sauté until browned on each side.

VEAL LOAF

(Makes 7–8 servings)

½ cup sour cream
1 small green pepper, chopped
4 carrots, chopped
1 small onion, chopped

2 teaspoons salt
⅛ teaspoon pepper
1 teaspoon paprika
2 pounds ground shoulder of veal

Preheat oven to 350 degrees F.

Put sour cream, green pepper, carrots, onion, salt, pepper and paprika in a blender container. Blend for 1 minute. Add mixture to ground veal. Mix thoroughly. Lightly pack meat mixture into an oiled loaf pan. Bake for 1½ hours.

Sauces for Meat

MARINARA SAUCE

(Makes about ½ quart)

⅓ cup olive oil
2 cloves garlic, minced
1 can (1 pound) Italian tomatoes
1 tablespoon chopped parsley

1 bay leaf
1½ teaspoons salt
¼ teaspoon pepper
⅛ teaspoon oregano
3 tablespoons tomato paste

Heat oil in a large, heavy saucepan. Add garlic, tomatoes, parsley, bay leaf, salt and pepper. Cook over low heat for 30 minutes. Add oregano and tomato paste. Cook for 15 minutes or until sauce thickens. Remove bay leaf.

PIZZAIOLA SAUCE

(Makes about ½ cup)

3 tablespoons olive oil	1 can (1 pound)
1 clove garlic, minced	Italian tomatoes
½ teaspoon salt	½ teaspoon oregano
¼ teaspoon pepper	1 tablespoon chopped
	parsley

Heat oil in a heavy skillet. Add garlic, salt, pepper and tomatoes. Cook over high heat for 20 minutes. Add oregano and parsley. Reduce heat and cook for 10 minutes more. Serve hot over fish, chops, steak or meat patties.

TOMATO SAUCE

(Makes about 1 quart)

4 tablespoons olive oil	1 can (28 ounces)
1 clove garlic, minced	Italian tomatoes
1 tablespoon chopped	¼ teaspoon basil
parsley	½ teaspoon oregano
1 onion, chopped	1 bay leaf
1 can (6 ounces)	¼ teaspoon salt
tomato paste	

Heat oil in a heavy skillet. Add garlic, parsley and onion. Cook for 10 minutes. Add remaining ingredients and simmer for 50 minutes. Remove bay leaf.

Vegetables

BEST EVER VEGETABLES

(Makes 2–3 servings)

1 tablespoon butter	1 (9 or 10 ounces)
Salt to taste	package frozen
Pepper to taste	vegetables

In a heavy skillet, combine all ingredients. Cover skillet. Cook over low heat until vegetables are tender. Shake skillet occasionally to prevent sticking.

DOUBLE BEANS AU GRATIN

(Makes 4 servings)

1 pound string beans, cooked and drained	⅓ cup grated Cheddar cheese
4 tomatoes, sliced	⅓ cup toasted crushed soybeans
Salt to taste	
Pepper to taste	⅓ cup butter

Preheat oven to 400 degrees F.

Place string beans in a buttered shallow baking dish. Arrange tomato slices over beans. Add salt and pepper. Sprinkle with cheese and soybeans. Dot with butter. Bake until cheese has melted.

ASPARAGUS ASPIC

(Makes 4 servings)

1 envelope unflavored
    gelatin
1½ cups cold water
3 tablespoons vinegar
1 teaspoon salt
½ teaspoon noncaloric
    liquid sweetener
⅛ teaspoon Tabasco
    sauce

1 cup cooked
    asparagus spears,
    cut up
1 tablespoon chopped
    parsley
1 tablespoon finely
    chopped celery
¼ cup diced pimento

Sprinkle gelatin over ½ cup cold water in saucepan.
Cook over low heat until gelatin is dissolved. Stir in
vinegar, salt, liquid sweetener, Tabasco and remaining
1 cup of water. Chill mixture until it begins to thicken.
Fold in remaining ingredients. Turn into a 3-cup mold.
Chill until firm. Unmold.

CAULIFLOWER PANCAKES

(Makes 4–6 servings)

1 small head
    cauliflower, cooked,
    drained and mashed
1 egg, slightly beaten
½ small onion, grated

Pepper to taste
2–4 tablespoons oat
    flour
Salad oil

In a bowl, combine all ingredients except oil and mix
well. In a heavy skillet, heat a few tablespoons of oil.
Drop spoonfuls of the mixture into the hot oil. Cook
pancakes on each side until crisp and browned. Add
more oil as needed.

BRAISED RED CABBAGE

(Makes 6 servings)

4 tablespoons bacon
  fat
1 small onion,
  chopped
2 sweet, unpeeled
  apples, cored and
  sliced
4 cups red cabbage,
  shredded

⅛ teaspoon ground
  ginger
⅛ teaspoon lemon rind
¾ teaspoon noncaloric
  liquid sweetener
2 tablespoons vinegar
½ teaspoon nutmeg
Salt to taste
Pepper to taste

Heat the bacon fat in a large skillet. Add onion and cook until golden. Add apples, cabbage, ginger, lemon rind, liquid sweetener, vinegar, nutmeg, salt and pepper. Cook over low heat until the cabbage is tender. Add a little water, if necessary, to keep the cabbage from sticking to the skillet.

CABBAGE AND SOUR CREAM

(Makes 4 servings)

3 tablespoons butter
1 small head cabbage,
  shredded
1 small onion, minced

½ teaspoon salt
¼ teaspoon paprika
1 cup sour cream

Preheat oven to 375 degrees F.

In a large, heavy skillet, heat butter. Add cabbage and onion. Sauté for 5 minutes. Season with salt and paprika. Butter a shallow baking pan. Spoon in vegetables. Top with sour cream. Bake for 25 minutes.

EGGPLANT WITH CHEESE

(Makes 4 servings)

3½ tablespoons butter
2 tablespoons anchovy paste
1 eggplant, pared and sliced
1 cup grated Cheddar cheese
¼ cup toasted soybeans, coarsely crushed

Preheat oven to 400 degrees F.

In a bowl, combine butter and anchovy paste thoroughly. Spread both sides of the eggplant slices with mixture. Place on a baking sheet. Sprinkle eggplant with grated cheese and soybeans. Bake for about 10 minutes or until tender.

SAUTEED EGGPLANT

(Makes 6 servings)

½ cup olive oil
1 large eggplant, peeled and cubed
1 onion, chopped
1 clove garlic, crushed
3 small tomatoes, chopped
1 can (6 ounces) tomato paste
Juice of 1 lemon
Salt to taste
Pepper to taste

In a large saucepan, heat oil. Add eggplant, onion and garlic. Cover pan and cook over medium heat for 10 minutes. Add tomatoes, tomato paste, lemon juice, salt and pepper. Simmer for 20 minutes.

MUSHROOMS AND EGGPLANT

(Makes 4 servings)

2 tablespoons butter
1 large onion, chopped
½ pound mushrooms, sliced

1 medium eggplant, peeled and cubed
½ cup bouillon
½ clove garlic, crushed
Salt to taste
Pepper to taste

In a saucepan, melt butter. Add onion. Cook until limp. Add mushrooms. Cook for 5 minutes. Add eggplant, bouillon, garlic, salt and pepper. Cover pan. Cook over low heat until vegetables are tender.

SOYBEANS AND TOMATOES

(Makes 4 servings)

1½ tablespoons butter
1½ cups soybeans, cooked or canned
¼ pound cooked bacon, chopped

¼ cup chopped onion
1 cup canned tomatoes
½ cup grated Cheddar cheese

Preheat oven to 350 degrees F.

Butter a baking dish. Cover bottom of dish with a layer of soybeans. Sprinkle with some of the bacon and onions. Repeat the process until all the beans are used up. Pour tomatoes over layered beans. Sprinkle with cheese. Bake for about 30 minutes, or until the top is browned.

OKRA AND EGGPLANT

(Makes 5 servings)

1 large eggplant, peeled and cubed
1 onion, sliced
4 small tomatoes, quartered

14 okra pods, sliced
Salt to taste
Pepper to taste

Combine all ingredients in a saucepan. Cover pan. Cook for 10–12 minutes over low heat until vegetables are tender.

SPINACH AU GRATIN

(Makes 4 servings)

1 (10 ounces) package frozen spinach, cooked and drained
¼ cup butter

½ teaspoon pepper
⅛ teaspoon nutmeg
3 tablespoons grated Cheddar cheese

In a saucepan, combine all ingredients thoroughly. Cover pan and cook over low heat until cheese melts.

BAKED SUMMER SQUASH

(Makes 4 servings)

3 cups summer squash, cut into strips
4 tablespoons butter

1 teaspoon salt
⅛ teaspoon pepper
¼ teaspoon paprika
¼ cup sour cream

Preheat oven to 350 degrees F.

Arrange squash in a buttered baking dish. Dot with butter, and sprinkle with salt, pepper and paprika. Pour cream over squash, and bake 15–20 minutes, or until tender.

SUMMER SQUASH IN SOUR CREAM

(Makes 4 servings)

2 tablespoons butter	Salt to taste
¼ cup chopped onion	½ teaspoon paprika
2 cups cooked summer squash, cubed	1 cup sour cream

Heat butter in a saucepan. Add onion and sauté for a few minutes. Add squash. Season with salt and paprika. Pour the sour cream over squash. Cook over low heat until thoroughly heated.

STRING BEANS AND MUSHROOMS WITH CREAM

(Makes 4 servings)

2 tablespoons butter	⅓ cup sour cream
1 cup mushrooms, sliced	½ teaspoon salt
2 cups cooked string beans, drained	⅛ teaspoon pepper

In a saucepan, melt butter. Add mushrooms and sauté for 5 minutes. Add string beans, sour cream, salt and pepper. Cover pan and cook until thoroughly heated.

SPINACH WITH BACON

(Makes 4 servings)

2 slices of bacon, cooked and crumbled

1½ cups cooked spinach, drained

¼ cup celery, finely chopped

4 anchovy fillets, chopped

4 tablespoons butter

Salt to taste

Pepper to taste

In a saucepan, combine bacon, spinach, celery and anchovies. Cook over low heat for 10 minutes. Add butter, salt and pepper. Mix well. Cook until thoroughly heated.

SPINACH CUSTARD

(Makes 4 servings)

2 cups cooked spinach, drained and chopped

2 tablespoons melted butter

2 eggs, slightly beaten

1 cup milk

6 drops noncaloric liquid sweetener

½ teaspoon chopped onion

⅛ teaspoon nutmeg

Salt to taste

Pepper to taste

1 teaspoon lemon juice

1½ tablespoons butter

Preheat oven to 300 degrees F.

In a bowl, combine all ingredients thoroughly. Butter a casserole. Pour in mixture. Bake until custard is firm, about 25–30 minutes.

ZUCCHINI AU GRATIN

(Makes 4 servings)

2 tablespoons butter
1 onion, sliced
1 pound zucchini,
  sliced
1 cup canned
  tomatoes
Salt to taste

Pepper to taste
½ cup grated
  Parmesan cheese
½ cup toasted
  soybeans, coarsely
  crushed

Preheat oven to 375 degrees F.

In a saucepan, melt butter. Add onion and sauté until limp. Add zucchini and cook for 5 minutes. Add tomatoes, salt and pepper. Cook for 5 minutes more. Remove from heat. Transfer mixture to a casserole. Sprinkle with cheese and soybeans. Bake until top is golden brown.

ZUCCHINI PANCAKES

(Makes 4–6 servings)

1½ pounds young
   zucchini, grated
   and drained
1 small onion, grated
1 egg, slightly beaten

1 teaspoon salt
4–6 tablespoons oat
   flour
Pepper to taste
Salad oil

In a bowl, combine all ingredients, except oil. Heat a few tablespoons of the oil in a heavy skillet. Drop spoonfuls of the mixture into the hot oil. Cook pancakes on each side until crisp and browned. Add more oil as needed.

STEWED TOMATOES

(Makes 6 servings)

2½ cups canned
   tomatoes
½ cup chopped celery
6 drops noncaloric
   liquid sweetener

¾ teaspoon salt
¼ teaspoon paprika
Soy granules

In a medium saucepan, combine all ingredients, except soy granules. Cover pan and cook for 10 minutes over medium heat. Add enough soy granules to liquid to thicken for desired consistency.

VEGETABLE STUFFING FOR FOWL

(Makes stuffing for large chicken or small turkey)

3 tablespoons salad
   oil
1 onion, chopped
1 green pepper,
   chopped
1 large eggplant,
   peeled and chopped
½ pound mushrooms,
   chopped

½ clove garlic, minced
¼ teaspoon basil
¼ teaspoon rosemary
¼ teaspoon thyme
Salt to taste
Pepper to taste
1 egg, well beaten
3 tablespoons soy
   flour

In a large, heavy skillet, heat the oil. Combine onion, green pepper, eggplant, mushrooms and garlic, and sauté until vegetables are tender. Add seasonings, soy flour and egg. Mix thoroughly. Remove from heat. Refrigerate until ready to use.

Salads

CHEF'S SALAD

(Makes 4 servings)

1 medium head
  lettuce, torn into
  bite-size pieces
1 avocado, peeled and
  sliced
2 tomatoes, cut into
  wedges
1 cup julienne cheese
  strips
1 cup julienne ham
  strips

4 hard-cooked eggs,
  sliced
⅓ cup salad oil
2 tablespoons lemon
  juice
⅛ teaspoon herb
  seasoning
¼ teaspoon salt
  Few grains pepper

Place greens in a large salad bowl. Arrange avocado, tomatoes, cheese, ham and eggs over greens. In a jar, combine oil, lemon juice, herb seasoning, salt and pepper. Before serving, shake covered jar to blend ingredients thoroughly. Pour dressing over salad. Toss salad gently and serve.

DINNER SALAD

(Makes 6–8 servings)

⅓ cup salad oil
¼ cup lemon juice
Few drops noncaloric
    liquid sweetener
¼ teaspoon salt
¼ teaspoon garlic salt
¼ teaspoon pepper
8 cups salad greens,
    torn into bite-size
    pieces

½ cup sliced red onion
    rings
¼ cup sliced radishes
½ cup coarsely
    shredded Cheddar
    cheese
8 ounces sliced
    boiled ham, cut into
    strips
½ cup toasted
    soybeans

Combine salad oil, lemon juice, liquid sweetener, salt, garlic salt and pepper in a jar with a tightly fitting cover. Close bottle and store in refrigerator while preparing salad. Arrange salad greens, onion rings, radish slices, cheese and ham attractively in a chilled salad bowl. Just before serving, sprinkle with soybeans. Shake dressing well and drizzle over salad. Toss gently, until all ingredients are coated with dressing.

EGG AND VEGETABLE SALAD

(Makes 6 servings)

2 cups shredded red
    cabbage
1 cup shredded raw
    carrots
½ cup sliced radishes
1 cucumber, sliced

1 teaspoon salt
⅛ teaspoon pepper
8 hard-cooked eggs,
    quartered
Mayonnaise

In a bowl, combine cabbage, carrots, radishes and cucumber. Season with salt and pepper. Serve in individual salad bowls topped with eggs and mayonnaise.

EGG AND SHRIMP SALAD

(Makes 6 servings)

3 quarts chilled salad greens
4 hard-cooked eggs, quartered
1 pound shrimp, cooked and cleaned
8–10 cherry tomatoes
1 cup sliced celery
¾ cup mayonnaise
¼ cup catsup
¼ cup chopped parsley
Lemon wedges

In a large bowl, tear salad greens into bite-sized pieces. Add eggs, shrimp, tomatoes and celery. Toss. In another bowl, combine mayonnaise and catsup. Pour over salad. Garnish with minced parsley and lemon wedges.

POTATO SALAD—HYPOGLYCEMIC'S STYLE

(Makes 6–8 servings)

4 cups Jerusalem artichokes, cooked, drained, and sliced
1 cup celery, diced
1 onion, minced
1 carrot, shredded
1 green pepper, cut into strips
1 cup mayonnaise
1 teaspoon salt
Pepper to taste

In a large bowl, combine all ingredients. Adjust seasonings. Chill until ready to serve.

CHICKEN BUTTERMILK LOAF

(Makes 3 servings)

1 envelope
unflavored gelatin
1 cup cold chicken
broth
½ cup buttermilk
1 tablespoon lemon
juice
½ teaspoon grated
lemon rind

¾ teaspoon salt
Few drops Tabasco
1 cup diced cooked
chicken
½ cup chopped celery
1 tablespoon chopped
parsley

Sprinkle gelatin over chicken broth in a saucepan and cook over low heat until gelatin is dissolved. Remove from heat. Stir in buttermilk, lemon juice, lemon rind, salt and Tabasco. Chill mixture until it begins to thicken. Fold in chicken, celery and parsley. Turn into a 2½-cup mold or small loaf pan. Chill until firm. Unmold.

BEAN POLE SALAD

(Makes 6 servings)

2 envelopes
unflavored gelatin
2½ cups cold water
1 tablespoon onion
flakes
½ cup tarragon
vinegar
1 tablespoon non-
caloric liquid
sweetener

1 teaspoon salt
½ cup chopped
pimento
1 can (1 pound)
whole green beans,
drained
1 can (4 ounces)
sliced mushrooms,
drained

Sprinkle gelatin over ½ cup cold water in saucepan. Stir in onion flakes. Place over low heat, stirring until gelatin is dissolved. Stir in remaining 2 cups of water, vinegar, liquid sweetener and salt. Chill mixture until it begins to thicken. Fold in pimento, beans and mushrooms. Turn into a 5-cup mold. Chill until firm. Unmold.

HOSTESS SALAD

(Makes 4 servings)

1 envelope (4-servings size) low-calorie lime flavor gelatin
⅛ teaspoon salt
1 cup boiling water
1 cup cold water
1 teaspoon lemon juice
Dash cayenne pepper
4 hard-cooked eggs, peeled

1 teaspoon prepared mustard
1 teaspoon vinegar
1 tablespoon milk
Dash salt and pepper
1 cup chopped celery
2 tablespoons chopped pimento
2 tablespoons chopped onion

In a bowl, dissolve gelatin and ⅛ teaspoon salt in boiling water. Add cold water, lemon juice and cayenne pepper. Chill until mixture begins to thicken. Meanwhile, halve eggs lengthwise. Reserve whites and mash yolks. In a bowl, combine egg yolks, mustard, vinegar, milk, salt and pepper. Fill whites with yolk mixture. Spoon just enough gelatin into a 1-quart ring mold to form a layer about ¼ inch thick. Arrange eggs, cut side down, on gelatin in mold. Add celery, pimento and onion to remaining gelatin. Spoon over eggs in mold. Chill until firm. Unmold on crisp lettuce.

SPANISH LAMB SALAD

(Makes 6 servings)

⅓ cup olive oil
¼ cup lemon juice
2 tablespoons vinegar
1 tablespoon chopped chives
½ teaspoon salt
½ teaspoon basil
⅛ teaspoon pepper
3 cups cooked lamb, slivered

½ cup sliced pimento-stuffed olives
1 small green pepper, sliced
2 medium tomatoes, diced
2 hard-cooked eggs, sliced
Lettuce

In a small bowl combine oil, lemon juice, vinegar, chives and seasonings. Mix well. Chill. Arrange lamb, olives, green pepper, tomatoes and eggs in lettuce-lined bowl. Pour dressing over all and toss gently.

CHICKEN AND TOMATO SALAD

(Makes 6 servings)

2 envelopes unflavored gelatin
10 ounces chicken broth
2 cups tomato juice
½ teaspoon salt
2 tablespoons lemon juice

¼ teaspoon Tabasco
2 cups diced cooked chicken
1 cup chopped celery
½ cup chopped cucumber
¼ cup sliced stuffed olives

Sprinkle gelatin over chicken broth in a saucepan. Place over low heat, stirring until gelatin is dissolved. Add tomato juice, salt, lemon juice and Tabasco. Chill,

stirring occasionally, until mixture begins to thicken.
Fold in diced chicken, celery, cucumber and olives.
Turn into a 6-cup mold. Chill until firm. Unmold onto
salad greens.

GARDEN SALAD

(Makes 5 servings)

1 envelope (4-
servings size) low-
calorie lemon flavor
gelatin
1 teaspoon salt
1 cup boiling water
1 cup cold water

4 teaspoons vinegar
⅔ cup sliced cucumber
½ cup thinly sliced
radishes
2 tablespoons
chopped scallions

In a bowl, dissolve gelatin and salt in boiling water.
Add cold water and vinegar. Chill until mixture begins
to thicken. Fold in vegetables. Pour into a 3-cup mold.
Chill until firm. Unmold.

CALIFORNIA STRAWBERRY SALAD

(Makes 4 servings)

1 large grapefruit,
peeled and sectioned
1 medium avocado,
peeled and sliced

2 pints fresh straw-
berries, washed
and hulled
Orange Cream Dressing
(recipe page 114)

Arrange grapefruit and avocado in a salad bowl. Top
with strawberries. Serve with chilled Orange Cream
Dressing.

HAM AND ORANGE SALAD

(Makes 3 servings)

1 envelope
(4-servings size)
low-calorie orange
flavor gelatin
¼ teaspoon salt
1 cup boiling water
1 cup cold water
1 teaspoon lemon
juice

1 cup diced ham
½ cup diced unpeeled
apple
½ cup diced orange
sections
⅛ teaspoon ground
cloves
⅛ teaspoon cinnamon

In a bowl, dissolve gelatin and salt in boiling water. Add cold water and lemon juice. Chill until mixture begins to thicken. Fold in ham, apple, orange sections and spices. Pour into a 3-cup mold. Chill until firm. Unmold on crisp greens.

GRAPEFRUIT COTTAGE CHEESE MOLD

(Makes 6 servings)

2 envelopes
unflavored gelatin
2½ cups canned
unsweetened
grapefruit juice
1 cup cream-style
cottage cheese
2 tablespoons
mayonnaise

½ teaspoon salt
1 tablespoon non-
caloric liquid
sweetener
1 cup canned
unsweetened
grapefruit sections,
halved

Sprinkle gelatin over ½ cup of the grapefruit juice in a saucepan. Cook over low heat until the gelatin is dissolved. Remove from heat. In a bowl, combine cottage cheese, mayonnaise, ¼ teaspoon salt and 1 tablespoon of the dissolved gelatin. Mix thoroughly. Turn into a 1½-quart mold. Chill until almost firm. Add remaining dissolved gelatin, salt, and liquid sweetener to remaining 2 cups of grapefruit juice. Chill mixture until it begins to set. Fold in the grapefruit sections. Spoon on top of almost firm cottage cheese layer. Chill until firm. Unmold. If desired, garnish with additional grapefruit sections.

VEGETABLE POP UPS

(Makes 32–36 cubes)

1 can (4 ounces) chopped mushrooms	½ cup finely chopped green pepper
2 envelopes unflavored gelatin	½ cup finely chopped cucumber
Cold water	½ cup finely chopped radishes
½ teaspoon noncaloric liquid sweetener	1 cup finely chopped cauliflower
1 teaspoon salt	1 cup finely chopped celery
¾ cup lemon juice	

Drain liquid from mushrooms into measuring cup. Add enough water to make 1 cup liquid. Pour into a saucepan and sprinkle gelatin over liquid. Cook over low heat, stirring until gelatin is dissolved. Remove from heat. Stir in 1½ cups cold water, liquid sweetener, salt and lemon juice. Chill, stirring occasionally, until mixture begins to thicken. Fold in vegetables. Spoon into 2 sectioned ice-cube trays. Chill until firm. Unmold and serve four cubes on individual lettuce-lined plates, or store cubes, covered, in refrigerator for snacking.

ORANGE AND GRAPEFRUIT STUFFED
LOBSTER TAIL

(Makes 1 serving)

5 ounces lobster tail, cooked

1 tablespoon catsup

1 tablespoon chopped celery

1 teaspoon chopped onion

1 tablespoon chopped green pepper

1 teaspoon salt

½ cup orange and grapefruit sections

Salad greens

Remove cooked meat from lobster tail, discarding cartilage. Reserve shell and set aside. In a bowl, chop lobster meat. Add catsup, celery, onion, chopped green pepper and salt. Mix well. Add fruit sections. Let mixture marinate at least ½ hour. Spoon into shell. Serve on salad greens.

Dressings

BLENDER MAYONNAISE

(Makes about 2 cups)

2 eggs	2 tablespoons vinegar
1½ cups salad oil	or lemon juice
½ teaspoon salt	½ teaspoon dry
⅛ teaspoon white	mustard
pepper	

In a blender container, put eggs, ½ cup oil, salt, pepper, vinegar and mustard. Cover container and turn motor to medium speed. While blender is on, add the remaining oil in a steady stream. As soon as all the oil is added, turn off motor. Store mayonnaise in a jar with a tight-fitting cover.

FRENCH DRESSING

(Makes about 2 cups)

½ cup cider vinegar   ½ teaspoon pepper
1 teaspoon salt   1½ cups salad oil

Combine all ingredients in a jar. Cover jar. Shake to blend before using.

ORANGE CREAM DRESSING

(Makes about 2 cups)

1 tablespoon non-   ½ cup orange juice
  caloric liquid   1 egg, well beaten
  sweetener   ¼ teaspoon salt
3 tablespoons lemon   ½ cup heavy cream,
  juice   whipped

In a saucepan, combine the liquid sweetener, lemon juice, orange juice, egg and salt. Cook over very low heat, stirring constantly, until mixture is thickened. Remove from heat. Transfer to bowl and chill thoroughly. Fold in whipped cream. Spoon over fruit salad.

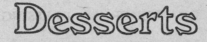

Desserts

BLUEBERRY PARFAIT

(Makes 4 servings)

½ cup cottage cheese	½ teaspoon lemon
¾ tablespoon non-caloric liquid sweetener	rind
	1 egg white
	Pinch of salt
½ cup heavy cream, whipped	1 pint blueberries, washed and drained

In a bowl, beat cottage cheese until smooth. Fold in liquid sweetener, whipped cream and lemon rind. Combine egg white and salt. Beat until stiff. Fold into the cottage cheese mixture. Alternate layers of the mixture and berries in parfait glasses. Chill until ready to serve.

117

FRESH FRUIT COMPOTE

(Makes 8 servings)

⅓ cup orange juice
¾ cup fresh ripe peach
    slices
¾ cup fresh ripe pear
    slices

1 cup cantaloupe
    melon balls
1 cup honeydew
    melon balls

In a bowl, combine all ingredients. Mix well. Spoon into compote or sherbert dishes. Chill.

FRUITED WHIPPED CREAM

(Makes 4 servings)

1 cup heavy cream
2 teaspoons fruit
    concentrate syrup

1 cup unsweetened
    canned or stewed
    fruit, drained

Combine heavy cream and fruit concentrate. Whip until thick. Fold in fruit. Spoon into parfait glasses. Chill in freezer for 10 minutes before serving.

PEACH FREEZE

(Makes 4 servings)

1 can (8 ounces)
    water-packed
    peaches, drained
1½ teaspoons non-
    caloric liquid
    sweetener

2 teaspoons lemon
    juice
½ teaspoon almond
    extract
2 egg whites
¼ teaspoon salt

In a blender container, combine peaches, liquid sweetener, lemon juice and almond extract. Blend until smooth. Combine egg whites and salt. Beat until stiff. Fold peach puree into egg whites. Pour into an icecube tray. Freeze until firm.

PINEAPPLE MOUSSE

(Serves 6–8)

1 can (1 pound, 4 ounces) unsweetened crushed pineapple

1 cup heavy cream, whipped

Place can of pineapple in freezer compartment until it is firm. Remove from freezer. Place pineapple in a chilled bowl. Break up fruit with a fork. Fold into whipped cream. Spoon into parfait glasses. Freeze again until ready to serve.

BAKED APPLES

(Makes 6 servings)

6 firm sweet apples
1 cup water
½ teaspoon noncaloric liquid sweetener

1 tablespoon cinnamon

Preheat oven to 350 degrees F.

Wash apples and core. Place in a shallow baking pan. In a small bowl, combine water, liquid sweetener and cinnamon. Mix thoroughly. Pour mixture over apples. Cover apples with aluminum foil. Bake 15 minutes. Remove foil. Baste apples with juices in pan frequently until tender.

STRAWBERRIES WITH PINEAPPLE AND CREAM

(Makes 8 servings)

1 medium pineapple
1 pint strawberries, washed and hulled
1 teaspoon orange extract
1 cup heavy cream

1½ teaspoons non-caloric liquid sweetener
½ cup unsweetened coconut, toasted

Cut pineapple in half, lengthwise. Scoop out meat. Reserve shells. Remove core and dice meat, discarding the core. Combine pineapple and strawberries and add orange extract. Chill. Combine cream and liquid sweetener. Beat cream until stiff. Fold into chilled fruit mixture. Mound in pineapple shells and sprinkle with coconut. Chill until ready to serve.

STRAWBERRY RICOTTA PARFAIT

(Makes 6 servings)

1 cup Ricotta cheese
1 cup mashed strawberries
1 teaspoon vanilla extract

Noncaloric liquid sweetener to taste
⅛ teaspoon salt
1 egg white
6 whole strawberries, washed and hulled

In a bowl, beat cheese until creamy and light. Add mashed strawberries, vanilla and liquid sweetener. Combine salt and egg white. Beat until stiff. Fold into cheese mixture. Spoon gently into parfait glasses and freeze until slightly firm.

STEWED BLUEBERRIES OR HUCKLEBERRIES

Wash berries carefully. Remove bits of leaf and stem. Place in saucepan. Add just enough water to keep them from burning. Cover and cook over low heat until soft. Sweeten to taste with noncaloric liquid sweetener.

May be used as filling for crêpes.
Folded into whipped cream as filling for a sponge cake or jelly roll. Combined with a small amount of unsweetened juice and used for pancake topping, etc.

CHOCOLATE SUPREME

(Makes 6–8 servings)

2 cups milk	¼ teaspoon salt
2 eggs, separated	5¼ teaspoons non-
1 envelope unflavored	caloric liquid
gelatin	sweetener
6 tablespoons Carob	1½ teaspoons vanilla
Powder mixed with	extract
4 tablespoons cold	½ cup heavy cream,
water *	whipped

* This mixture equals 2 ounces unsweetened chocolate.

In a saucepan, combine milk, egg yolks, gelatin, Carob mix, ⅛ teaspoon salt and liquid sweetener. Cook over very low heat, stirring constantly until gelatin is dissolved and mixture is thick enough to coat a spoon. Remove from heat and stir in vanilla. Chill until mixture begins to thicken. Combine remaining salt and egg whites. Beat until stiff. Fold Carob mixture into stiffly beaten egg whites. Fold in whipped cream. Gently spoon mixture into a 4-cup mold. Chill until firm. Unmold and serve.

CHOCOLATE SATIN

(Makes 6 servings)

2 envelopes unflavored gelatin	1 tablespoon non-caloric liquid sweetener
3 cups milk	1/8 teaspoon salt
6 tablespoons Carob Powder mixed with 4 tablespoons cold water *	1/2 teaspoon vanilla extract
	1 cup heavy cream, whipped

* This mixture equals 2 ounces unsweetened chocolate.

In a saucepan, sprinkle gelatin over milk. Cook over low heat, stirring constantly until gelatin is dissolved. Add Carob mix. Stir until it is mixed. Remove from heat. Add liquid sweetener, salt and vanilla. Beat until smooth. Chill until mixture begins to thicken. Beat until light and fluffy. Pour into a 4-cup mold. Chill until firm. Garnish with whipped cream.

COCONUT CHIFFON CREAM

(Makes 6–8 servings)

3 eggs, separated	1 tablespoon non-caloric liquid sweetener
2 cups milk	1/4 teaspoon salt
1/2 cup unsweetened shredded coconut	1 1/2 teaspoons vanilla extract
1 envelope unflavored gelatin	

In a saucepan, combine egg yolks, 1 cup milk, coconut, gelatin, liquid sweetener and 1/8 teaspoon salt. Mix well. Cook over very low heat, stirring constantly until gelatin is dissolved. Remove from heat and let mixture stand for 20 minutes. Add remaining milk. Chill until mixture begins to thicken. Combine remaining salt, egg whites and vanilla. Beat until stiff. Fold coconut mixture into the egg whites. Spoon carefully into a 6-cup mold. Chill until firm. Unmold and serve.

CHEESE RING WITH STRAWBERRIES

(Makes 10 servings)

1 package (8 ounces) cream cheese, softened
5 egg yolks
1 teaspoon grated lemon peel
2 tablespoons lemon juice

2 tablespoons non-caloric liquid sweetener
1 envelope unflavored gelatin
¼ teaspoon salt
1 cup light cream
1 pint sour cream
3 pints strawberries, washed and hulled

In a large mixing bowl, combine cheese, egg yolks, lemon peel, lemon juice and liquid sweetener. Beat until light and fluffy. Set aside. Combine gelatin, salt, light cream and sour cream in the top of a double boiler. Mix well. Cook over hot water until gelatin is dissolved. Remove from heat and gradually stir 1 cup of the gelatin mixture into the cheese mixture. Return all to top of double boiler. Place over simmering water and stir constantly for 2 minutes. Pour into a 6-cup ring mold. Cool. Chill until firm. Unmold onto a serving plate. Pile strawberries into center of mold and serve.

FRUIT MOUSSE

(Makes about 8–10 servings)

1 cup fruit pulp,
sweetened with
noncaloric liquid
sweetener to taste

⅛ teaspoon salt

½ cup cold water

1½ teaspoons non-
caloric liquid
sweetener

1¼ teaspoons
unflavored gelatin

1 pint heavy cream,
whipped

In a bowl, combine fruit pulp and salt. Set aside. In a saucepan, combine remaining ingredients, except cream. Mix well. Cook over low heat, stirring constantly, until gelatin is dissolved. Remove from heat and add fruit pulp. Mix well. Pour into an ice-cube tray. Freeze until partially set. Remove to a bowl and beat until light and fluffy. Fold in whipped cream. Return to tray and freeze until firm.

LEMON ICE

(Makes 6 servings)

1 envelope low-calorie
lemon flavor gelatin

1 cup boiling water

1½ cups cold water

2 teaspoons non-
caloric liquid
sweetener

½ cup lemon juice

1 teaspoon grated
lemon rind

In a bowl dissolve gelatin in boiling water. Add cold water and remaining ingredients. Pour into a shallow pan and freeze until almost firm. Remove to chilled bowl and beat until smooth. Freeze again until firm.

LEMON CHIFFON FREEZE

(Makes 6 servings)

3 eggs, separated
½ cup lemon juice
4 teaspoons non-
   caloric liquid
   sweetener

1 envelope unflavored
   gelatin
2 cups cold water
⅛ teaspoon salt
½ cup toasted
   almonds, chopped

In a saucepan, combine egg yolks, lemon juice, liquid sweetener, gelatin, and cold water. Cook over very low heat, stirring constantly, until gelatin dissolves. Chill the mixture until it begins to thicken. In a bowl, combine salt and egg whites. Beat until stiff. Fold lemon mixture into the egg whites. Sprinkle chopped nuts over bottom of a 4-cup mold. Pour in the lemon mixture. Freeze until firm. Unmold on a platter.

GREEN PINEAPPLE JELL

(Makes 6 servings)

1 envelope low-calorie
   lime flavor gelatin
2 cups boiling water
2 cans (6 ounces each)
   unsweetened
   pineapple juice

1 can (8 ounces)
   unsweetened crushed
   pineapple
1 cup heavy cream,
   whipped

In a bowl, combine gelatin and water. Stir until gelatin is dissolved. Add pineapple juice and pineapple. Mix well. Chill until mixture begins to thicken, stirring occasionally. Pour into 6 dessert cups. Chill until firm. Serve with whipped cream.

ORANGE SOUFFLE

(Makes 6 servings)

1¼ cups cold water
2 envelopes
   unflavored gelatin
1 can (6 ounces)
   undiluted frozen
   orange juice
1 cup Ricotta cheese

1 egg, separated
½ teaspoon lemon rind
1 teaspoon orange
   rind
¼ teaspoon salt
2 cups orange sections

In a saucepan, sprinkle gelatin over water. Cook over low heat until gelatin is dissolved. Add orange juice. Mix well. Set aside. In a bowl, combine cheese and egg yolk. Beat until light and creamy. Add lemon and orange rind and gelatin mixture. Chill until mixture begins to thicken. Combine salt and egg white. Beat until stiff. Fold egg white into cheese mixture. Arrange orange sections in bottom of a 4-cup mold. Spoon in cheese mixture. Chill until firm. Unmold and serve.

PARTY CHOCOLATE LOAF

(Makes 10–12 servings)

1 cup milk
6 tablespoons Carob
   Powder mixed with
   2 tablespoons cold
   water *
2 eggs, separated
¼ teaspoon salt
2 envelopes
   unflavored gelatin

3 tablespoons non-
   caloric liquid
   sweetener
3 cups Ricotta cheese,
   sieved
1 teaspoon vanilla
   extract
1 cup heavy cream,
   whipped

* This is a substitute for ½ cup cocoa.

Combine milk, Carob mix, egg yolks, ⅛ teaspoon salt, gelatin and liquid sweetener in a saucepan. Cook over very low heat, stirring constantly, until gelatin dissolves and mixture is smooth. Remove from heat and add cheese and vanilla. Mix well. Chill mixture until it begins to thicken. In a bowl, combine remaining salt and egg whites. Beat until stiff. Fold in the cheese mixture. Fold in the whipped cream. Spoon into a loaf pan. Chill until firm. Unmold and serve.

PINEAPPLE-CHEESE MOLD

(Makes 6–8 servings)

1 envelope unflavored gelatin

1 cup unsweetened pineapple juice

1 package (8 ounces) cream cheese, softened

2 teaspoons non-caloric liquid sweetener

1 teaspoon vanilla extract

½ cup instant nonfat dry milk

½ cup ice water

2 tablespoons lemon juice

In a saucepan, sprinkle gelatin over pineapple juice. Cook over low heat, stirring until gelatin is dissolved. Remove from heat. In a bowl, beat cheese until smooth. Add liquid sweetener and vanilla. Mix well. Add gelatin mixture a little at a time, mixing well after each addition. Chill until thickened. Combine dry milk and ice water in a chilled bowl. Beat until soft peaks form. Add lemon juice. Beat until stiff. Fold gelatin mixture into stiffly beaten milk. Spoon gently into a 4-cup mold. Chill until firm. Unmold and serve.

PEACH PARFAIT

(Makes 3 servings)

1 envelope unflavored gelatin
¼ cup cold water
1¼ cups buttermilk
1 tablespoon lemon juice
1 tablespoon non-caloric liquid sweetener
¾ teaspoon almond extract
Yellow food coloring
2 peaches, sliced

In a saucepan, sprinkle gelatin over water. Cook over low heat until gelatin is dissolved. Remove from heat. Add buttermilk, lemon juice, liquid sweetener, almond extract and a few drops of yellow food coloring. Mix well. Chill mixture until it begins to thicken. Layer gelatin mixture and peaches in 3 parfait glasses, using about ⅔ cup gelatin mixture in each glass. Chill until firm.

ORANGE WHIP

(Makes 8 servings)

1 envelope unflavored gelatin
¼ cup cold water
1 cup boiling water
¼ teaspoon salt
1 can (6 ounces) frozen undiluted orange juice
2 egg whites
Orange sections

In a bowl, sprinkle gelatin over cold water. Add boiling water and salt and stir until gelatin is dissolved. Add orange juice and mix well. Chill mixture until it begins to thicken. Beat egg whites until stiff. Fold in the orange mixture. Spoon into dessert dishes. Garnish with orange sections. Chill until firm.

SPANISH CREAM

(Makes 4 servings)

2 eggs, separated	1 envelope unflavored
2 cups milk	gelatin
2¼ teaspoons non-	1 teaspoon vanilla
caloric liquid	extract
sweetener	¼ teaspoon salt

Beat egg yolks slightly. In a saucepan, combine egg yolks, 1 cup milk, liquid sweetener and gelatin. Cook over low heat, stirring constantly, until gelatin is dissolved. Add remaining milk and vanilla. Mix well. Chill until mixture begins to thicken. Combine egg whites and salt. Beat until stiff. Fold gelatin mixture into stiffly beaten egg whites. Spoon into a 4-cup mold. Chill until firm. Unmold and serve.

PINEAPPLE-APRICOT FREEZE

(Makes 6 servings)

2 cans (12 ounces each) low-calorie apricot nectar	1 can (1 pound, 4 ounces) unsweetened crushed pineapple
1 envelope unflavored gelatin	3 egg whites, stiffly beaten

In a saucepan, sprinkle gelatin over 1 can of apricot nectar. Cook over low heat, stirring constantly until gelatin is dissolved. Remove from heat. Add remaining nectar and pineapple. Mix well. Pour into ice-cube tray. Freeze for ¾ hour. Turn frozen mixture into a bowl. Beat until mixture is fluffy. Fold in egg whites. Return to tray. Freeze until firm.

COFFEE CHEESE SPONGE

(Makes 6 servings)

1 envelope unflavored gelatin

¼ cup cold decaffeinated coffee

1 tablespoon vanilla extract

1⅛ teaspoons noncaloric liquid sweetener

1 cup hot decaffeinated coffee

1¼ cups cottage cheese, sieved

2 egg yolks, beaten

3 egg whites

¼ teaspoon salt

1 cup heavy cream, whipped (optional)

In a bowl, sprinkle gelatin over cold coffee. Add vanilla, liquid sweetener and hot coffee. Stir until gelatin is dissolved. Cool. Blend cottage cheese and egg yolks. Add coffee mixture and beat thoroughly. Combine egg whites and salt. Beat until stiff. Fold into the cheese mixture. Spoon into a 1½-quart mold. Chill until firm. Unmold and garnish with whipped cream.

PINEAPPLE-LEMON SPONGE

(Makes 8 servings)

2 envelopes unflavored gelatin

½ cup unsweetened pineapple juice

1 cup boiling water

4½ teaspoons non-caloric liquid sweetener

⅛ teaspoon salt

½ teaspoon grated lemon rind

½ cup lemon juice

1¾ cups cold water

2 egg whites

In a bowl, sprinkle gelatin over ¼ cup pineapple juice.

Add boiling water and stir until gelatin is dissolved. Add liquid sweetener, salt, lemon rind, remaining pineapple juice, lemon juice and cold water. Mix well. Chill until mixture begins to thicken. Beat with electric beater until mixture is frothy. Beat egg whites until stiff. Fold in gelatin mixture. Pour into a 4-cup mold. Chill until firm. Unmold.

SKY HIGH STRAWBERRY SOUFFLE

(Makes 6 servings)

1 pint strawberries, washed, hulled and sieved

2 tablespoons plus 1½ teaspoons non-caloric liquid sweetener

1 envelope unflavored gelatin

4 eggs, separated

⅛ teaspoon salt

1 cup heavy cream, whipped

Cut a strip of waxed paper about 4 inches wide and long enough to go around the outside of a 1½-quart soufflé dish. Place waxed paper around the outside of soufflé dish so that it forms a 2-inch collar above the rim. Fasten with string. Lightly brush inside surface of collar with salad oil. Combine strawberries and 1 tablespoon of liquid sweetener in a bowl. Remove ¼ cup of the sweetened puree and sprinkle gelatin over top. Set aside. Combine egg yolks with 1 tablespoon liquid sweetener in top part of a double boiler. Stir over boiling water until thickened. Add gelatin mixture and stir until gelatin is dissolved. Cool. Add remaining strawberry puree and mix well. Combine egg whites, salt and 1½ teaspoons liquid sweetener. Beat until stiff. Fold in whipped cream, then strawberry mixture. Pour into prepared soufflé dish. Chill until firm. Remove collar and serve.

STRAWBERRY APPLESAUCE WHIP

(Makes 8 servings)

2 envelopes low-
    calorie, strawberry
    flavor gelatin
2 cups boiling water
2 cups unsweetened
    applesauce

¼ teaspoon nutmeg
¼ teaspoon mace
2 egg whites
1 pint strawberries,
    washed, hulled and
    sliced

In a bowl, dissolve gelatin in boiling water. Add applesauce, nutmeg, and mace. Mix well. Chill until mixture
begins to thicken. Beat egg whites until stiff. Fold into
applesauce mixture. Spoon into sherbert glasses. Chill.

STRAWBERRY BAVARIAN CREAM

(Makes 6 servings)

1 envelope unflavored
    gelatin
1 tablespoon non-
    caloric liquid
    sweetener
⅛ teaspoon salt
2 eggs, separated
1¼ cups milk

1 pint fresh straw-
    berries, washed,
    hulled and sliced
1 teaspoon vanilla
    extract
1 cup heavy cream,
    whipped

In a saucepan, combine gelatin, liquid sweetener, salt,
egg yolks and milk. Cook over very low heat, stirring
constantly, until mixture is thick enough to coat a
spoon. Cool. Add strawberries and vanilla. Chill mixture until it begins to thicken. Beat egg whites until
stiff. Fold into gelatin mixture. Fold in whipped cream.
Spoon into a 1½-quart mold. Chill until firm. Unmold
and garnish with additional strawberries, if desired.

VANILLA PUDDING

(Makes 4–5 servings)

2 cups milk
2 eggs, lightly beaten
⅛ teaspoon salt
1 envelope unflavored gelatin

1 tablespoon non-caloric liquid sweetener
1½ teaspoons vanilla extract

Combine milk, eggs, salt, gelatin and liquid sweetener in a saucepan. Cook over low heat, stirring constantly, until mixture is thick enough to coat a spoon. Remove from heat. Add vanilla. Pour into custard cups. Chill until firm.

Variation
Add 1 tablespoon instant coffee granules and cook as directed. Substitute 1 teaspoon of coffee extract for the vanilla.

LEMON FROST

(Makes 6 servings)

2 eggs, separated
1½ teaspoons non-caloric liquid sweetener
¼ cup lemon juice

½ teaspoon grated lemon rind
⅛ teaspoon salt
½ cup heavy cream, whipped

In a bowl, beat egg yolks until thick and lemon-colored. Add liquid sweetener, lemon juice and ¼ teaspoon lemon rind. Continue beating for 5 minutes. Combine salt and egg whites and beat until stiff. Fold in egg-yolk mixture. Fold in whipped cream. Spoon into parfait glasses. Garnish with remaining lemon rind. Freeze until firm.

BAKED CUSTARD

(Makes 5 servings)

3 eggs, beaten
2 teaspoons non-caloric liquid sweetener

⅛ teaspoon salt
1 teaspoon vanilla extract
2 cups milk, scalded

Preheat oven to 325 degrees F.

In a bowl, combine eggs, liquid sweetener, salt and vanilla. Mix thoroughly. Gradually add milk, stirring constantly. Pour into buttered custard cups. Place cups in a pan of hot water. Bake for 45 minutes, or until knife inserted near center comes out clean. Chill.

TORTONI

(Makes 8 servings)

1 cup heavy cream
2 teaspoons non-caloric liquid sweetener
1 tablespoon instant decaffeinated coffee granules
1½ teaspoons vanilla extract

¼ teaspoon almond extract
1 egg white
⅛ teaspoon salt
½ cup chopped toasted almonds
¼ cup shredded unsweetened coconut, toasted

In a bowl, combine cream, liquid sweetener, coffee granules, vanilla and almond extract. Whip until stiff. Combine egg white and salt. Beat until stiff and fold into whipped cream. Fold in ¼ cup chopped almonds and coconut. Spoon mixture into small dessert cups. Sprinkle with remaining almonds.

PUMPKIN CUSTARD

(Makes 6–8 servings)

4 teaspoons non-caloric liquid sweetener
¼ teaspoon salt
1½ teaspoons cinnamon
¼ teaspoon nutmeg
⅛ teaspoon cloves
⅛ teaspoon ground ginger
1 can (1 pound) pumpkin
3 eggs, lightly beaten
¾ cup evaporated milk
¼ cup milk

Preheat oven to 425 degrees F.

Combine all ingredients in a bowl. Mix well. Pour into buttered custard cups. Bake for 15 minutes. Reduce heat to 400 degrees. Bake 30 minutes more, or until a knife inserted into the center comes out clean. Chill and serve.

VANILLA ICE CREAM

(Makes 6–8 servings)

6 eggs, separated
1 cup milk
2 cups heavy cream
4½ teaspoons non-caloric liquid sweetener
1½ teaspoons vanilla extract
¼ teaspoon salt

Beat egg yolks slightly. Combine egg yolks, milk and 1 cup heavy cream in a saucepan. Cook over low heat, stirring constantly, until mixture is thickened. Add liquid sweetener and cool. In a bowl, combine egg whites and salt. Beat until stiff. Fold into egg-yolk mixture. Whip remaining cream and fold into mixture. Place in ice-cube tray and freeze.

STRAWBERRY PUDDING

(Makes 6–8 servings)

3 egg yolks, slightly beaten
2 cups milk
2 tablespoons strawberry concentrate syrup
1 tablespoon non-caloric liquid sweetener
1 envelope unflavored gelatin
¼ teaspoon salt
3 egg whites
1 teaspoon vanilla extract
2 cups strawberries, washed, hulled and sliced

In a saucepan, combine egg yolks, milk, strawberry concentrate, liquid sweetener, gelatin and ⅛ teaspoon salt. Cook over very low heat, stirring constantly, until mixture is thick enough to coat a spoon. Remove from heat. Add vanilla. Chill until mixture begins to thicken. In a bowl, combine remaining salt and egg whites. Beat until stiff. Fold in egg-yolk mixture. Fold in strawberries. Spoon into individual dessert dishes. Chill until firm.

CREAM CHEESE CUSTARD

(Makes 6 servings)

1 package (8 ounces) cream cheese
3 eggs, separated
3½ teaspoons non-caloric liquid sweetener
2 teaspoons vanilla extract
1 tablespoon lemon juice
½ teaspoon lemon rind
1 cup sour cream
½ teaspoon vanilla extract

Preheat oven to 350 degrees F.

Combine cream cheese, egg yolks, 2 teaspoons liquid sweetener, 2 teaspoons vanilla, lemon rind and lemon juice in a blender container. Blend until smooth. Beat egg whites until stiff. Fold into cheese mixture. Pour into an 8-inch pie pan and bake for 25 minutes. Combine sour cream, 1½ teaspoons liquid sweetener, ½ teaspoon vanilla and spread over the surface. Return to oven and bake for 5 minutes more. Chill.

Cakes
and
Cookies

ALMOND ROLL

(Makes 10 servings)

7 eggs, separated	1/8 teaspoon salt
4½ teaspoons non-caloric liquid sweetener	1½ cups grated almonds
	1½ cups heavy cream
2 teaspoons almond extract	Almond extract
	Noncaloric liquid sweetener
1 teaspoon baking powder	Toasted slivered almonds

Preheat oven to 350 degrees F.

Oil a jelly roll pan and line with waxed paper. Oil the paper and set aside. Combine egg yolks, liquid sweetener and almond extract in a bowl. Beat until thick and lemon-colored. Add baking powder and continue beating for 3 minutes. Combine salt and egg whites and beat until stiff. Fold egg-yolk mixture into stiffly beaten egg whites. Fold in almonds. Spoon into the prepared pan. Bake for 15 minutes. Invert pan onto a slightly dampened towel. Remove pan and peel off waxed paper. Roll up cake and towel. Cool. Whip cream and flavor with almond extract and liquid sweetener. Unroll cake and spread evenly with cream and sprinkle with toasted almonds. Roll up cake and chill for at least 1 hour before serving.

SPONGE CAKE LAYERS

(2 8-inch cakes)

10 eggs, separated
1 tablespoon lemon juice
1 tablespoon vanilla extract
2 tablespoons non-caloric liquid sweetener

¼ teaspoon salt
2½ teaspoons baking powder
1 cup oat flour, sifted
¼ teaspoon cream of tartar

Preheat oven to 350 degrees F.

Oil bottom of 2 8-inch layer-cake pans. Line bottoms with waxed paper. Oil paper and set aside. In a bowl, combine egg yolks, lemon juice, vanilla, liquid sweetener, salt and baking powder. Beat until thick and lemon-colored. Combine egg whites and cream of tartar. Beat until stiff. Fold egg-yolk mixture into stiffly beaten egg whites. Fold in oat flour by thirds. Spoon into prepared pans. Bake for 35 minutes. Remove from oven and let cake cool in pans. Invert pans and remove paper.

JELLY ROLL

6 eggs, separated
2 teaspoons pineapple extract
2 teaspoons grated lemon rind
1½ tablespoons non-caloric liquid sweetener

¼ cup unsweetened pineapple juice
1 cup sifted oat flour
⅛ teaspoon salt
1½ teaspoons baking powder
1½ cups filling (custard, whipped cream, or pureed fruit)

Preheat oven to 350 degrees F.

Oil a jelly roll pan and line with waxed paper. Oil the paper. Set pan aside. In a bowl, combine egg yolks, pineapple extract, lemon rind, liquid sweetener and pineapple juice. Beat until thick and lemon-colored. Combine dry ingredients. Beat egg whites until stiff. Fold egg-yolk mixture into stiffly beaten egg whites. Sift dry ingredients over mixture, folding in as you sift. Spoon into prepared pan. Bake for 18 minutes. Invert pan onto a slightly dampened towel. Remove pan and peel off paper. Roll up cake and towel. Cool. Unroll cake and spread evenly with desired filling. Roll up cake and serve.

BANANA CAKE

(Makes 1 loaf)

2 cups oat flour	2 eggs, well beaten
1 cup skim milk powder	1 cup mashed bananas
¾ teaspoon baking soda	2 tablespoons non-caloric liquid sweetener
1¼ teaspoons cream of tartar	
¼ teaspoon salt	1 teaspoon vanilla extract
½ cup coarsely chopped nuts	⅓ cup melted butter

Preheat oven to 350 degrees F.

In a bowl, combine oat flour, skim milk powder, baking soda, cream of tartar, salt and chopped nuts. In another bowl, combine eggs, bananas, liquid sweetener and vanilla. Beat well. Add the butter and mix well. Add dry ingredients and blend thoroughly. Pour into a 3½-x10½-inch buttered loaf pan. Bake for 45–50 minutes. Cool and serve.

STRAWBERRY SPONGE CAKE

(Makes 1 8-inch cake)

2 pints strawberries,
    washed and hulled
3 teaspoons non-
    caloric liquid
    sweetener
¼ cup strawberry fruit
    concentrate

2 cups heavy cream
1½ teaspoons vanilla
    extract
2 8-inch Sponge Cake
    layers (recipe page
    142)

Reserve ½ pint whole strawberries for garnish. Slice
remaining strawberries. In a bowl, combine sliced
strawberries, 1 teaspoon liquid sweetener and strawberry concentrate. Chill for 30 minutes. Combine heavy
cream, 2 teaspoons liquid sweetener and vanilla. Beat
until stiff. Place 1 cake layer on a serving plate. Spread
with whipped cream and strawberry mixture. Top with
second layer. Spread remaining cream on top and sides
of cake. Garnish top of cake with whole strawberries.
Chill until ready to serve.

EASY CHEESE CAKE

(Makes 8 servings)

Sweet Pastry (recipe
    page 162)
4 eggs, separated
3½ teaspoons non-
    caloric liquid
    sweetener
2 cups pot cheese
¼ teaspoon salt

½ teaspoon lemon
    extract
1 teaspoon grated
    lemon rind
1 cup heavy cream
¼ cup sifted oat flour
¼ teaspoon cream of
    tartar

Preheat oven to 300 degrees F.

Line bottom of an 8-inch spring-form pan with pastry. Chill until ready to use. Combine egg yolks, 2 teaspoons liquid sweetener, pot cheese, salt, lemon extract and lemon rind in a blender container. Blend until smooth. Add cream and oat flour. Blend 1 minute. In a bowl, combine egg whites, cream of tartar and 1½ teaspoons liquid sweetener. Beat until stiff. Fold cheese mixture into the stiffly beaten egg whites. Pour into prepared pan. Bake for 1 hour. Turn off heat. Leave cake in oven for 1 hour with oven door closed. Remove from oven and chill before serving.

LEMON REFRIGERATOR CHEESECAKE

(Makes 10–12 servings)

¾ cup lemon juice
2 envelopes unflavored gelatin
¼ teaspoon salt
¼ cup cold water
2 eggs, separated
1½ teaspoons grated lemon rind
3 tablespoons non-caloric liquid sweetener
¼ teaspoon lemon extract
3 cups cottage cheese, sieved
1 cup heavy cream, whipped

Combine lemon juice, gelatin, ⅛ teaspoon salt, water, egg yolks, lemon rind and liquid sweetener in a saucepan. Cook over low heat, stirring constantly, until gelatin is dissolved. Chill until mixture begins to thicken. Fold in lemon extract and cottage cheese. Set aside. In a bowl, combine remaining salt and egg whites. Beat until stiff. Fold cheese mixture into the egg whites. Fold in whipped cream. Spoon into a 9-inch lightly oiled spring-form pan. Chill until firm. Unmold and serve.

COCOA ROLL

(Makes 8–10 servings)

8 eggs, separated
2 tablespoons non-caloric liquid sweetener
2 teaspoons vanilla extract
¼ teaspoon salt

9 tablespoons of Carob Powder mixed with 4 tablespoons cold water *
¼ teaspoon cream of tartar
½ cup unsweetened coconut meal
1 cup heavy cream, whipped

* This is a substitute for 6 tablespoons cocoa.

Preheat oven to 350 degrees F.

Oil a jelly roll pan and line with waxed paper. Oil the paper and set aside. Beat egg yolks until thick and lemon-colored. Add liquid sweetener, vanilla, salt and Carob mixture. Continue beating for 5 minutes. In another bowl, combine cream of tartar and egg whites. Beat until stiff. Gently fold Carob mixture into stiffly beaten egg whites. Fold in coconut meal. Spoon mixture into prepared pan. Bake for 12 minutes. Invert pan onto a slightly dampened towel. Remove pan and peel off waxed paper. Roll cake and towel. Cool. Unroll cake and spread with whipped cream. Roll and refrigerate until ready to serve.

PARTY STRAWBERRY CHEESECAKE

(Makes 16 servings)

2 envelopes (4-servings size) low-calorie strawberry flavor gelatin

1 cup water

2 egg yolks, slightly beaten

3 cups cottage cheese, sieved

2 egg whites, stiffly beaten

1 cup heavy cream, whipped

8 strawberries, halved

¼ cup ground walnuts

1 tablespoon butter, melted

⅛ teaspoon cinnamon

⅛ teaspoon nutmeg

Line bottom of a 9-inch spring-form pan with waxed paper. Combine gelatin and water in a heavy saucepan. Cook over low heat until gelatin is dissolved. Stir small amount of hot mixture into egg yolks. Mix well. Add yolks to gelatin mixture in pan. Cook over low heat, stirring constantly, for 1 minute. Combine gelatin mixture and cheese in a large bowl. Mix well. Fold in the stiffly beaten egg whites. Fold in whipped cream. Arrange strawberry halves, cut side up, on bottom of pan. Pour cheese mixture over berries. Combine walnuts, butter and spices. Sprinkle over top of cheese mixture. Chill until firm, at least 3 hours. Unmold onto a serving platter. Carefully remove waxed paper from cake.

WALNUT ROLL

(Makes 8 servings)

5 eggs, separated
1 teaspoon vanilla
extract
1 teaspoon walnut
extract
1 teaspoon noncaloric
liquid sweetener
1½ teaspoons baking
powder

¾ cup grated walnuts
¼ teaspoon cream of
tartar
1½ cups heavy cream
1 teaspoon vanilla
extract
¼ cup finely chopped
walnuts

Preheat oven to 350 degrees F.

Oil a jelly roll pan and line with waxed paper. Oil the paper and set pan aside. In a bowl, beat egg yolks until thick and lemon-colored, gradually adding the vanilla, walnut extract, liquid sweetener and baking powder. Beat 1 minute more. Add grated walnuts. Mix well. Combine egg whites and cream of tartar. Beat until stiff. Fold egg-yolk mixture into the stiffly beaten egg whites. Spoon mixture into prepared pan. Bake for 12–15 minutes. Invert pan onto a slightly dampened towel. Remove pan and peel off waxed paper. Roll up cake and towel. Cool. Combine heavy cream and vanilla. Beat until stiff. Fold in walnuts. Unroll cake and spread evenly with whipped-cream mixture. Roll up. Refrigerate until ready to serve.

STRAWBERRY-CHEDDAR CHEESECAKE

(Makes 8 servings)

Sweet Pastry (recipe page 162)
2 tablespoons melted butter
2 packages (8 ounces each) cream cheese, softened
½ cup shredded Cheddar cheese
4½ teaspoons non-caloric liquid sweetener

3 eggs
½ teaspoon grated orange rind
¼ teaspoon grated lemon rind
2 tablespoons oat flour
1 cup heavy cream
1 pint strawberries, washed and hulled

Preheat oven to 350 degrees F.

Line the bottom of a 9-inch spring-form pan with pastry. Bake for 5 minutes. Remove from oven and set aside. In a bowl combine cream cheese, Cheddar cheese and liquid sweetener. Beat until light and fluffy. Add eggs, 1 at a time, beating well after each addition. Add orange and lemon rind, oat flour and ½ cup cream. Mix well. Pour into prepared pan. Bake for 40 minutes, or until cake is set in the center. Remove from oven and cool. Arrange strawberries on top of the cake, stem side down. Whip remaining cream until stiff. Decorate top of cake with whipped cream.

MERINGUE KISSES

(Makes about 12)

3 egg whites
⅛ teaspoon salt
1 tablespoon non-
    caloric liquid
    sweetener

1 teaspoon almond
    extract
½ cup unsweetened
    shredded coconut
½ cup grated almonds

Preheat oven to 250 degrees F.

In a bowl, combine egg whites, salt, liquid sweetener and almond extract. Beat until stiff. Fold in coconut and almonds. Drop by spoonfuls onto a buttered cookie sheet. Bake for 30 minutes. Turn off oven heat. Leave in oven with door closed for 30 minutes.

SPONGE CAKE

(1 loaf)

5 large eggs, separated
2 tablespoons non-
    caloric liquid
    sweetener
1 teaspoon orange
    extract
2 tablespoons grated
    orange rind
¼ teaspoon cream of
    tartar

1 cup oat flour, sifted
⅛ teaspoon salt
2½ teaspoons baking
    powder
2 tablespoons
    undiluted frozen
    orange juice
    concentrate
1 teaspoon cold water

Preheat oven to 325 degrees F.

Oil bottom of a 3½-x10½-inch loaf pan and line with waxed paper. Oil paper and set aside. In a bowl, combine egg yolks, liquid sweetener, orange extract and orange rind. Beat until thick and lemon-colored. Add oat flour, salt and baking powder. Mix well. Add orange juice and water. Mix well. Add cream of tartar to egg whites and beat until stiff. Fold egg-yolk mixture into the stiffly beaten egg whites. Pour into prepared pan. Bake for 70 minutes, or until tester comes out dry when inserted into center of cake. Remove from oven and cool cake in pan.

SPECIAL CHEESECAKE

(Makes 10 servings)

Sweet Pastry dough
    (recipe page 162)
6 eggs, separated
5 teaspoons non-
    caloric liquid
    sweetener
1¾ cup sour cream
1½ pounds cream
    cheese, softened

2 tablespoons oat
    flour
1½ teaspoons vanilla
    extract
2 teaspoons grated
    lemon rind
1 tablespoon lemon
    juice
¼ teaspoon cream of
    tartar

Preheat oven to 325 degrees F.

Line the bottom of a 9-inch spring-form pan with pastry and chill. Combine egg yolks, liquid sweetener and sour cream in a blender container. Blend for 2 minutes. Add cream cheese, oat flour, vanilla, lemon rind and lemon juice. Blend until smooth. In a bowl, combine egg whites and cream of tartar. Beat until stiff. Fold cheese mixture into egg whites. Pour into prepared pan. Bake for 65 minutes. Turn off heat, leaving cake to cool with oven door open.

COCONUTTY COOKIES

(Makes about 12)

½ cup oat flour
1 egg, slightly beaten
½ cup unsweetened
   shredded coconut
¼ cup peanut butter

⅛ teaspoon salt
1 teaspoon noncaloric
   liquid sweetener
1½ teaspoons vanilla
   extract

Preheat oven to 350 degrees F.

In a bowl, combine all ingredients. Mix well. Chill for 1 hour. Form dough into balls about walnut size. Place on a greased cookie sheet. Press with a flat-bottom glass to form circles. Bake for 12–15 minutes.

OATMEAL COOKIES

(Makes about 3 dozen cookies)

1 cup oat flour
1 cup oatmeal
1 teaspoon baking
   powder
½ teaspoon baking
   soda
⅛ teaspoon salt
1½ teaspoons cinnamon
½ cup chopped
   walnuts

⅛ teaspoon nutmeg
¼ pound butter,
   melted
1 egg, well beaten
1 tablespoon non-
   caloric liquid
   sweetener
2 tablespoons milk

Preheat oven to 350 degrees F.

In a bowl, combine dry ingredients. Add butter and blend thoroughly with a fork. Add liquid sweetener and egg. Mix well. Add milk, 1 tablespoon at a time, blending well after each addition. Form dough into small balls the size of a walnut. Place on a greased cookie sheet. Press with a flat-bottom glass to form circles ⅛ inch thick. Bake for 15 minutes.

STRAWBERRY CHEESECAKE

(Makes 12–14 servings)

Sweet Pastry (recipe page 162)

5 packages (8 ounces each) cream cheese, softened

3 tablespoons plus 1½ teaspoons non-caloric liquid sweetener

3 tablespoons oat flour

1 tablespoon grated lemon rind

1 teaspoon vanilla extract

¼ cup milk

6 eggs

1 pint strawberries, washed and hulled

½ cup strawberry fruit concentrate

Preheat oven to 350 degrees F.

Line the bottom of a 9-inch spring-form pan with pastry. Bake for 5 minutes. Remove from oven and set aside. In a large mixing bowl, combine cheese, liquid sweetener, oat flour, lemon rind, vanilla and milk. Beat until smooth. Add eggs, one at a time, beating well after each addition. Pour mixture into prepared pan. Bake for 15 minutes. Reduce heat to 250 degrees F. and bake for 1 hour longer. Turn off heat and allow cake to cool in oven with door open for about 3 hours. Arrange strawberries, stem side down, on top of cake. Cook fruit concentrate over low heat, until slightly thickened. Remove from heat and cool slightly. Spoon over strawberries. Chill before serving.

PEANUT BUTTER COOKIES

1 cup oatmeal	1 cup peanut butter
1 cup oat flour	4 tablespoons butter, melted
1½ teaspoons cinnamon	
¼ teaspoon salt	2 tablespoons milk
1 teaspoon baking powder	2 teaspoons non-caloric liquid sweetener
½ teaspoon baking soda	2 eggs, well beaten

Preheat oven to 350 degrees F.

In a bowl, combine dry ingredients. Cut in peanut butter with a pastry blender or 2 knives. Add butter, milk, liquid sweetener and eggs. Mix thoroughly. Chill for 30 minutes. Form dough into small balls the size of a walnut. Place on a greased cookie sheet. Press with a flat-bottom glass to form circles ⅛ inch thick. Bake for 18 minutes.

CINNAMON SQUARES

(Makes 35–40 squares)

2 cups oatmeal	Juice of 1 lemon
¼ pound butter, melted	Grated rind of 1 lemon
2 ounces chopped walnuts	1 tablespoon non-caloric liquid sweetener
¼ teaspoon salt	2 eggs, well beaten
4 tablespoons cinnamon	Walnut halves

Preheat oven to 400 degrees F.

In a large mixing bowl, combine oatmeal, butter, nuts, salt, cinnamon, lemon juice, lemon rind and liquid sweetener. Mix well. Add eggs and blend thoroughly. Butter a shallow 7½- x 12-inch baking dish. Spread dough in pan evenly. Place walnut halves about 1 inch apart, pressing into dough slightly. Bake 35–40 minutes. Cut into squares while hot. Store in a covered jar in refrigerator.

CHOCOLATE COOKIES

4 cups quick-cooking oatmeal	2 tablespoons non-caloric liquid sweetener
½ pound sweet butter, melted	9 tablespoons Carob Powder mixed with 4 tablespoons cold water *
¼ teaspoon salt	
2 tablespoons vanilla extract	1 can (13 ounces) evaporated milk
1 tablespoon almond extract	4 eggs, well beaten
4 ounces chopped walnuts	

* This mixture is equal to 3 ounces unsweetened chocolate.

Preheat oven to 350 degrees F.

In a large bowl, combine oatmeal, butter, salt, vanilla, almond extract, walnuts, liquid sweetener, Carob mixture and milk. Mix well. Add eggs. Blend well. Pour into 2 buttered shallow baking pans. Bake for 35 minutes. Remove pans from oven. Cool. Cut into small squares. Store in a covered jar in the refrigerator.

Fillings and Toppings

LEMON FROSTING OR FILLING

(Makes enough for 2 layers or 1 jelly roll)

2 tablespoons lemon juice

2 egg yolks, lightly beaten

1½ teaspoons non-caloric liquid

1 teaspoon lemon rind

¾ cup heavy cream, whipped

Combine lemon juice, egg yolks and liquid sweetener in a saucepan. Cook over low heat, stirring constantly, until mixture is thick enough to coat a spoon. Cool thoroughly. Fold lemon rind and whipped cream into cooled mixture. Frost or fill cake layers. Refrigerate until ready to serve.

CUSTARD SAUCE

(Makes about 2½ cups)

4 eggs, lightly beaten

¼ teaspoon salt

2 cups milk

4 teaspoons noncaloric liquid sweetener

1 teaspoon almond extract

Combine eggs, salt, milk and liquid sweetener in a saucepan. Cook over very low heat, stirring constantly, until slightly thickened. Remove from heat and add almond extract. Chill. Serve over sliced fruit or sliced cake.

JELLY ROLL FILLING AND FROSTING

(Makes enough for 1 jelly roll)

1 envelope unflavored gelatin

2 tablespoons cold water

2 tablespoons instant decaffeinated coffee granules

¾ cup warm milk

3 eggs, separated

4 teaspoons non-caloric liquid sweetener

¾ cup heavy cream, whipped

In a bowl, sprinkle gelatin over water. In a saucepan combine coffee granules, milk, egg yolks, liquid sweetener and gelatin. Cook over low heat, stirring constantly, until mixture is slightly thickened and gelatin is dissolved. Chill mixture until it begins to thicken. Fold in whipped cream. Beat egg whites until stiff. Fold into mixture. Chill until firm enough to spread.

PINEAPPLE CAKE TOPPING

(Topping for 1 cake)

1 teaspoon unflavored gelatin

¼ cup cold unsweetened pineapple juice

¼ cup hot unsweetened pineapple juice

½ cup drained unsweetened crushed pineapple

In a bowl, sprinkle gelatin over cold juice. Add hot juice and stir until gelatin is dissolved. Chill until syrupy. Add crushed pineapple. Spread over cooled cake. Chill until topping is firm.

SOUR CREAM CAKE SAUCE

(Makes about 2 cups)

1 teaspoon vanilla
    extract
1 cup sour cream
⅜ teaspoon non-
    caloric liquid
    sweetener

1 cup sliced fruit or
    berries

In a bowl, combine all ingredients. Blend well. Spoon over cake slices or custard.

WHIPPED CREAM CAKE FILLING

(Makes enough for a 2-layer cake)

1½ teaspoons
    unflavored gelatin
2 tablespoons cold
    water
½ cup light cream
2 egg yolks, lightly
    beaten
2¼ teaspoons non-
    caloric liquid
    sweetener

½ cup heavy cream,
    whipped
1 teaspoon almond
    extract
½ teaspoon vanilla
    extract
½ cup blanched,
    toasted, slivered
    almonds

In a bowl, sprinkle gelatin over water. Heat the light cream in a saucepan until it begins to simmer. Combine egg yolks and liquid sweetener and gradually add to hot light cream, stirring until thick. Add gelatin. Cook mixture over low heat, stirring constantly, until gelatin is dissolved. Remove from heat. Cool. Fold whipped cream, almond extract, vanilla and almonds into cooled mixture. Chill until thick enough to spread.

Pies

PLAIN PASTRY

(Makes 1 8- or 9-inch pie shell)

1 egg
¼ teaspoon salt
1 cup oat flour

3 tablespoons butter, melted

In a bowl, combine egg, salt, oat flour and butter. Mix thoroughly. (Dough will be a little sticky.) Chill for 30 minutes. Roll out dough between two sheets of waxed paper to fit an 8- or 9-inch pie plate. Dough may be pressed to fit pie plate.

Note: To make a baked pie shell, line a pie plate with pastry. Set another pan inside to hold the pastry in shape. Bake at 425 degrees F. for 18 minutes.

BRAZIL NUT PIE CRUST

1¼ cups Brazil nuts, ground
1 tablespoon non-caloric liquid sweetener

2 tablespoons oat flour
⅛ teaspoon salt
2 tablespoons melted butter

Preheat oven to 375 degrees F.
In a bowl, combine all ingredients thoroughly. Chill for 30 minutes. Press mixture to fit an 8-inch pie plate. Bake for 10–12 minutes. Cool.

SWEET PASTRY

(Makes 1 8- or 9-inch pie shell)

1 egg, slightly beaten	1 teaspoon almond extract
1 tablespoon non-caloric liquid sweetener	¾ cup oat flour
¼ teaspoon salt	¼ cup grated almonds
	3 tablespoons butter, melted

In a bowl, combine ingredients. Mix thoroughly. Chill for 30 minutes. Roll out dough between two sheets of waxed paper to fit an 8- or 9-inch pie plate. Dough may be pressed to fit pie plate.

Note: To make a baked pie shell, line a pie plate with pastry. Set another pan inside to hold pastry in shape. Bake at 425 degrees F. for 18 minutes.

ALMOND CUSTARD PIE

(Makes about 8 servings)

Sweet Pastry (recipe above)	¼ teaspoon salt
2 tablespoons butter	1 teaspoon vanilla extract
1 cup blanched almonds, chopped	½ teaspoon almond extract
4 eggs, lightly beaten	2½ cups milk, scalded
1 tablespoon non-caloric liquid sweetener	

Preheat oven to 400 degrees F.

Line a 9-inch pie plate with pastry. Melt butter in a saucepan. Add almonds and brown lightly. Sprinkle almonds over bottom of pastry. Chill until ready to use. In a bowl, combine eggs, liquid sweetener, salt, vanilla and almond extract. Slowly pour milk into mixture, stirring constantly. Pour mixture into prepared pie plate. Bake for about 25–30 minutes, or until knife inserted into center comes out clean. Remove from oven and cool. Refrigerate until ready to serve.

APRICOT CHIFFON PIE

(Makes 6–8 servings)

4½ teaspoons unflavored gelatin

2 tablespoons low-calorie apricot nectar

3 eggs, separated

1 teaspoon non-caloric liquid sweetener

½ cup low-calorie apricot nectar

⅛ teaspoon salt

1 tablespoon lemon juice

1 can (1 pound) water-packed apricots, drained and mashed

1 8-inch Sweet Pastry Pie Shell (recipe page 162)

In a saucepan, combine gelatin, apricot nectar, egg yolks, liquid sweetener and salt. Cook over low heat, stirring constantly, until gelatin is dissolved. Remove from heat. Add apricots and lemon juice. Mix well. Chill until mixture begins to thicken. Combine egg whites and salt. Beat until stiff. Fold apricot mixture into stiffly beaten egg whites. Spoon lightly into baked pie shell. Chill until firm.

BLUEBERRY CREAM PIE

(Makes 6–8 servings)

4 eggs
1 tablespoon non-caloric liquid sweetener
1 teaspoon vanilla extract
¼ teaspoon salt
1 envelope unflavored gelatin
¼ cup cold water
1 cup heavy cream, whipped
1¼ cups blueberries, drained and mashed
1 8-inch baked pie shell

In a bowl, beat eggs until frothy. Add liquid sweetener, vanilla and salt. Mix well. In a saucepan, sprinkle gelatin over cold water. Cook over low heat until gelatin is dissolved. Stir gelatin gradually into egg mixture. Fold in whipped cream. Chill until mixture begins to thicken. Carefully fold in blueberries. Spoon mixture into baked pie shell. Chill until firm.

COTTAGE CHEESE PIE

(Makes 6–8 servings)

Plain Pastry (recipe page 161)
4 eggs, separated
¼ cup heavy cream
1 tablespoon non-caloric liquid sweetener
¼ teaspoon salt
1 teaspoon vanilla extract
1 pound cottage cheese
1 teaspoon grated lemon rind
¼ cup lemon juice

Preheat oven to 450 degrees F.

Line an 8-inch pie pan with pastry. Set aside. In a blender container, combine egg yolks, heavy cream, liquid sweetener, salt, vanilla and cottage cheese. Blend until smooth. Add lemon rind and lemon juice. Blend 1 minute. In a bowl, beat egg whites until stiff. Fold stiffly beaten egg whites into cheese mixture. Pour filling into the prepared pan. Bake for 10 minutes. Reduce heat to 350 degrees F. and bake 35 minutes more or until filling is firm. Chill.

CHERRY CHIFFON PIE

(Makes 6–8 servings)

1 envelope unflavored gelatin

½ cup plus 2 tablespoons cherry juice

3 eggs, separated

⅛ teaspoon salt

4½ teaspoons noncaloric liquid sweetener

1 can (1 pound) unsweetened cherries, drained

1½ teaspoons lemon rind

1 8-inch pie crust, baked

In a saucepan, sprinkle gelatin over cherry juice. Add egg yolks, salt and liquid sweetener. Cook over low heat, stirring constantly, until gelatin is dissolved and mixture coats a spoon. Chill until mixture begins to thicken. Add cherries and lemon rind. Beat egg whites until stiff. Fold into cherry mixture. Spoon lightly into baked pie crust. Chill until firm.

BLUEBERRY YOGURT PIE

(Makes 6–8 servings)

1 package (8 ounces) cream cheese, softened

¾ teaspoon lemon extract

1 teaspoon grated lemon rind

1 tablespoon non-caloric liquid sweetener

1 cup plain yogurt

1½ cups blueberries, washed and drained

1 8-inch pie crust, baked

In a bowl, combine cream cheese, lemon extract, lemon rind, liquid sweetener and yogurt. Beat mixture until very smooth. Gently fold in blueberries. Spoon lightly into baked pie crust. Chill until firm.

JIFFY PINEAPPLE CHEESE PIE

(Makes 6–8 servings)

1 package (8 ounces) cream cheese, softened

1 cup heavy cream, whipped

1½ teaspoons non-caloric liquid sweetener

1 can (1 pound, 4 ounces) unsweetened crushed pineapple

½ teaspoon pineapple extract

1 8-inch pic shell, baked

In a bowl, beat cream cheese until light and fluffy. Fold in whipped cream and liquid sweetener. Add pineapple and pineapple extract. Spoon into the baked pie shell. Chill until filling is firm.

APRICOT CREAM PIE

(Makes 6–8 servings)

1 envelope unflavored gelatin
¼ cup cold water
2 tablespoons lemon juice
1 tablespoon non-caloric liquid sweetener
¼ teaspoon salt
2 cans (6 ounces each) low-calorie apricot nectar
½ cup heavy cream, whipped
1 8-inch pie crust, baked

In a saucepan, sprinkle gelatin over water. Add lemon juice, liquid sweetener, salt and apricot nectar. Cook over low heat, stirring occasionally, until gelatin is dissolved. Chill until mixture begins to thicken. Fold whipped cream into gelatin mixture. Spoon lightly into baked pie crust. Chill until firm.

NO CRUST CHEESE PIE

(Makes 6–8 servings)

1 pound cream cheese
½ cup light cream
1 tablespoon non-caloric liquid sweetener
2 eggs
2 teaspoons vanilla extract
½ cup sour cream
1 cup strawberries, washed and hulled

Preheat oven to 350 degrees F.

In a blender container, combine cream cheese, light cream, liquid sweetener, eggs and vanilla. Blend until completely smooth. Pour into an 8-inch pie plate. Bake for 25 minutes. Open oven door and let pie cool. Chill. Garnish with sour cream and strawberries.

RASPBERRY CHIFFON PIE

(Makes 6–8 servings)

1 envelope unflavored
    gelatin
¼ cup cold water
1 tablespoon lemon
    juice
3 eggs, separated
4 teaspoons noncaloric
    liquid sweetener

⅛ teaspoon salt
2½ cups raspberries,
    washed and sieved
1 8-inch pie crust,
    baked

In a saucepan, combine gelatin, water, lemon juice, egg yolks, liquid sweetener and salt. Cook over low heat, stirring constantly, until gelatin is dissolved and mixture coats a spoon. Remove from heat and add raspberries. Chill until mixture begins to thicken. In a bowl, beat egg whites until stiff. Fold into fruit mixture. Spoon lightly into baked pie crust. Chill until firm.

BLUEBERRY CHIFFON PIE

(Makes 6–8 servings)

1 envelope unflavored
    gelatin
¼ cup cold water
3 eggs, separated
2 tablespoons non-
    caloric liquid
    sweetener
½ cup lemon juice

1 teaspoon lemon
    rind
⅛ teaspoon salt
1½ cups blueberries,
    washed and drained
Pinch of salt
1 8-inch pie crust,
    baked

In a saucepan, sprinkle gelatin over water. Add egg yolks, liquid sweetener, lemon juice, lemon rind and salt. Cook over low heat, stirring constantly, until gelatin is dissolved and mixture coats a spoon. Chill until mixture begins to thicken. Beat egg whites until stiff. Fold stiffly beaten egg whites and blueberries into gelatin mixture. Spoon mixture lightly into baked pie crust. Chill until firm.

PINEAPPLE CHIFFON PIE

(Makes 6–8 servings)

3 eggs, separated	1½ teaspoons non-caloric liquid sweetener
1 tablespoon lemon juice	¼ teaspoon salt
1 can (1 pound, 4 ounces) unsweetened crushed pineapple	1 8-inch pie shell, baked
1 envelope plus 1 teaspoon unflavored gelatin	

In a saucepan, beat egg yolks until frothy. Add lemon juice, pineapple, gelatin, liquid sweetener and ⅛ teaspoon of salt. Cook over low heat, stirring constantly, until gelatin is dissolved. Remove from heat. Chill mixture until it begins to thicken. Add remaining salt to egg whites. Beat until stiff. Carefully fold pineapple mixture into egg whites. Spoon mixture into baked pie shell. Chill until firm.

LEMON CHIFFON CREAM PIE

(Makes 6–8 servings)

1 envelope unflavored gelatin
2 tablespoons cold water
⅔ cup milk
3 eggs, separated
4 teaspoons non-caloric liquid sweetener
¼ cup lemon juice
2 teaspoons lemon rind
½ cup heavy cream, whipped
1 8-inch pie crust, baked

In a saucepan, sprinkle gelatin over water. Add milk, egg yolks, liquid sweetener, lemon juice and lemon rind. Mix thoroughly. Cook over low heat, stirring constantly, until gelatin is dissolved and mixture coats a spoon. Chill until mixture begins to thicken. Beat egg whites until stiff. Fold into gelatin mixture. Fold in whipped cream. Spoon lightly into baked pie crust. Chill until firm.

DEEP DISH APPLE PIE

(Makes 6–8 servings)

1 cup quick-cooking oatmeal
½ teaspoon baking soda
⅓ cup butter
⅓ cup water
1½ teaspoon grated lemon rind
5 sweet apples, peeled and cut into eighths
1½ teaspoons cinnamon
½ teaspoon nutmeg
2 teaspoons lemon juice
½ teaspoon ground ginger

Preheat oven to 375 degrees F.

In a bowl, combine oatmeal and baking powder. Gradually cut in butter until mixture is crumbly. Add water and lemon rind. Work mixture into paste. Arrange apples in a buttered baking dish. Sprinkle with cinnamon, nutmeg, lemon juice and ginger. Spread the oatmeal paste over the apples. Bake for about 45 minutes or until pastry is well browned.

STRAWBERRY CREAM PIE

(Makes 6–8 servings)

2 pints strawberries, washed and hulled	3 egg whites
	¼ teaspoon salt
2 tablespoons non-caloric liquid sweetener	1 cup heavy cream, whipped
½ cup cold water	1 8-inch pie shell, baked
2 envelopes unflavored gelatin	½ cup heavy cream, whipped (optional)

Slice enough strawberries to make 3 cups. Set the rest aside. Combine sliced strawberries and 1 tablespoon liquid sweetener. Let stand a few minutes, then mash. In a small pan, sprinkle gelatin over cold water and cook over low heat until gelatin is dissolved. Stir gelatin into sliced strawberries. Chill, stirring occasionally. Remove from refrigerator when mixture begins to thicken. Combine egg whites, salt and remaining liquid sweetener. Beat until stiff. Fold whites into strawberry mixture. Fold in 1 cup heavy cream, whipped. Spoon lightly into baked pie shell. Chill until firm. Garnish with remaining strawberries and, if desired, whipped cream.

STRAWBERRY CHIFFON PIE

(Makes 6–8 servings)

1 envelope unflavored gelatin
¼ cup cold water
3 eggs, separated
1 tablespoon lemon juice
4½ teaspoons non-caloric liquid sweetener
⅛ teaspoon salt

1 cup strawberry pulp and juice
1 8-inch pie crust, baked
1 cup heavy cream, whipped
1 cup strawberries, washed, hulled and drained

In a saucepan, sprinkle gelatin over water. Add egg yolks, lemon juice, liquid sweetener and salt. Cook over low heat, stirring constantly, until gelatin is dissolved and mixture coats a spoon. Add strawberry pulp and juice. Chill until mixture begins to thicken. Beat egg whites until stiff. Fold into strawberry mixture. Spoon gently into baked pie crust. Chill until firm. Garnish with whipped cream and strawberries.

MOM'S APPLE PIE

(Makes 6–8 servings)

Plain Pastry (recipe page 161)
7 sweet apples, cored, peeled, and sliced
⅛ teaspoon ground ginger
⅛ teaspoon nutmeg
1 tablespoon cinnamon

1 teaspoon lemon juice
1 teaspoon lemon rind
1 tablespoon butter
Noncaloric liquid sweetener to taste
Cheddar cheese (optional)

Preheat oven to 400 degrees F.

Line an 8-inch pie plate with pastry. Set aside. In a large bowl, combine apples, ginger, nutmeg, cinnamon, lemon juice, lemon rind, butter and liquid sweetener. Spoon into prepared pie plate. Cover apples with aluminum foil. Seal by turning foil under ridge of pie plate. Make slits in top of foil to let steam escape. Bake for 30 minutes. Remove foil and bake 20 minutes more. Serve warm with slices of Cheddar cheese.

STRAWBERRY MOUSSE PIE

(Makes 6–8 servings)

1 pint fresh strawberries, washed and hulled	1 tablespoon lemon juice
4½ teaspoons non-caloric liquid sweetener	½ cup heavy cream, whipped
1½ tablespoons unflavored gelatin	2 egg whites
¼ cup cold water	⅛ teaspoon salt
½ cup boiling water	1 8-inch pie shell, baked
	½ cup heavy cream, whipped (optional)

Reserve a few strawberries for garnish; cut the remainder in half and puree in an electric blender with 1 tablespoon of liquid sweetener. Strain thoroughly to remove seeds. Sprinkle gelatin over cold water. Add boiling water and stir until gelatin is dissolved. Add lemon juice and strawberry puree. Chill mixture until it begins to thicken. Fold in whipped cream. Combine egg whites, salt and 1½ teaspoons liquid sweetener. Beat until stiff. Fold into strawberry mixture. Spoon mixture into baked pie shell. Chill until firm. Garnish with reserved strawberries and additional whipped cream, as desired.

Beverages

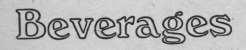

BANANA BREAKFAST IN A GLASS

(Makes 1 serving)

1 cup milk
1 egg
½ banana

¼ teaspoon vanilla
    extract

In a blender container, combine all ingredients. Cover container and blend until smooth. Serve cold.

FRUIT COCKTAIL COOLER

(Makes 1 serving)

¼ cup unsweetened
    grapefruit juice
¼ cup orange juice,
½ teaspoon lemon
    juice

Noncaloric liquid
    sweetener to taste
½ cup club soda
Crushed ice

Combine all ingredients in a glass. Add desired amount of crushed ice.

ORANGE BREAKFAST IN A GLASS

(Makes 1 serving)

½ cup milk   ½ cup orange juice
1 egg

In a blender container, combine all ingredients. Cover
container and blend until smooth. Serve cold.

STRAWBERRY CUSTARD COOLER

(Makes about 6 servings)

4 eggs, lightly beaten   1 teaspoon vanilla
1 tablespoon non-   extract
   caloric liquid   4 teaspoons straw-
   sweetener   berry concentrate
¼ teaspoon salt   1 cup strawberries,
3 cups milk, scalded   washed, hulled, and
                                 drained

Blend eggs, liquid sweetener and salt in a saucepan.
Stir hot milk slowly into mixture. Blend thoroughly.
Cook over low heat, stirring constantly, until mixture
coats a spoon. Pour into a chilled bowl. Add vanilla
and strawberry concentrate. Mix well. Cover bowl and
refrigerate. Before serving, put custard, milk and strawberries into a blender container. Blend for ½ minute.
Pour into chilled glasses.

FRUIT PUNCH

(Makes about 25 servings)

¾ cup strawberry
concentrate
3½ cups orange juice
1 cup lemon juice
1 cup weak tea
1 cup unsweetened
pineapple juice

1½ cups water
Noncaloric liquid
sweetener to taste
1 quart club soda
Ice

In a large punch bowl, combine strawberry concentrate, orange juice, lemon juice, tea, pineapple juice, water and liquid sweetener. Mix well. Chill thoroughly. Before serving, add club soda and ice.

HOT SPICED APPLE PUNCH

(Makes 5 servings)

1 cup apple juice
2¾ cups water
1 stick cinnamon

12 whole cloves
1 envelope low-calorie
orange flavor gelatin
2 teaspoons lemon
juice

In a covered saucepan, simmer apple juice, water, cinnamon and cloves for 10 minutes. Strain. Dissolve the flavored gelatin in the hot liquid. Add lemon juice. Serve hot.

MAPLE-FLAVORED BREAKFAST IN A GLASS

(Makes 1 serving)

1 cup milk, chilled
1 egg
1 teaspoon instant
   decaffeinated coffee
   granules

1 teaspoon maple-
   flavored extract

In a blender container, combine all ingredients. Cover container and blend ingredients until frothy. Pour into a tall glass. Serve immediately.

Useful
Hints

Artificial Sweeteners. Buy any type you like. Use the equivalent of the amount used in any of the recipes calling for sweeteners.

Bread. If your doctor permits you bread, buy high protein bread only. Some breads are made with soy flour, artichoke flour or oat flour. (Don't eat more bread than is allowed. In fact, it is best if you don't eat bread at all.)

Canned Fruit. Buy canned fruits that are packed in water, or frozen fruits with no sugar added. Canned pineapple comes now packed in its own juice too, with no sugar added.

Canned Vegetables. Read label. Many have sugar added.

Chocolate. Should your hypoglycemia be very mild and should your doctor permit you chocolate in small quantities, buy only unsweetened baking chocolate. It contains only 7.7 grams of carbohydrate per ounce and only a trace of caffeine.

Coffee. Decaffeinated only, of course. Use any brand you like—instant or ground. When perking Sanka, add some Franc's chicory for better flavor.

Cold Cuts. Read label. Many packaged cold cuts contain dextrose or corn syrup.

Corn Oil. Do not use in any form. It is often found in salad dressings, margarine, etc. Buy margarine made from soy or cottonseed oil.

Custards. Use a wire whisk. Cook over very low heat, stirring constantly. NOTE: Having a wire whisk is essential for keeping custards, gravies, etc., free of lumps.

Desserts. You may safely add more or less artificial sweetener than a recipe calls for. Prepare dessert and pie recipes in double quantity; they can be eaten on alternate days for desserts or for snacks.

"Dietetic" Products. Many contain some form of starch or carbohydrates. Don't buy an item just because it is labeled "dietetic." Also note that "natural sweetener added" may mean sugar added.

Eggs. Always use large eggs. All recipes call for large eggs unless otherwise specified.

Flavoring Extracts. May be purchased in many fruit flavors, which are available in most department stores. Supermarkets generally carry vanilla, orange and almond flavors.

Gravy. Thicken with a small amount of oat flour and cold water, blending both with a wire whisk to avoid lumps.

Instant Breakfasts. Don't buy any of the instant breakfast products; they may contain some form of sugar. Breakfast drinks such as Tang or Orange Plus contain sugar also. Serve only unsweetened juices—canned, frozen or fresh.

Juice Drinks. Don't buy canned drinks labeled "juice drink." They are usually made with sugar, water and a little fruit juice.

Oat Flour. Although oat flour can be purchased, it may be more convenient to make your own. Put quick-cooking oats in a blender container. Cover and blend till fine. Sift once to remove large particles. Store flour in a covered container. If you are just beginning treatment for hypoglycemia, do not eat large portions of the recipes calling for oat flour or macaroni.

Pies, Cheese Cakes. Chiffon pies can be made without using a crust. Just put pie filling into pie pan and chill. Serve in wedges. The same goes for cheese cakes: Just pour the batter into baking pan and bake. And serve in wedges.

Pie Crusts. Use oat flour. (One cup of oat flour equals approximately 3½ ounces.)

Potatoes. If your doctor permits you potatoes, cook only a small one for yourself. Baked potatoes may be enriched with cheese: Scoop out the inside, mash and add butter and some cheese. Put all this back into the shell and broil till top is brown.

Salad Dressings. Try to make your own. The bottled ones may contain sugar or may be made with corn oil.

Seasoning Products. Read label. Most bottled or packaged seasoning products contain some type of starch or sugar.

Yogurt. Don't buy fruit-filled yogurt. Buy plain yogurt and add fresh or water-packed fruit.

• • •

You will find in your local health food store:
   Fruit concentrate syrup (no sugar added)
   Bouillon and meat flavorings to make broths
   Pastas in all shapes and forms made from Jerusalem
      artichoke flour
   Water-packed fruits
   Oat flour (But see note above.)
   Soy products: toasted soy beans (salted and
      unsalted); cooked and canned soy beans; raw soy
      beans; soy flour
   Macaroni, spaghetti, and noodles made from and
      mixed with artichoke flour (DeBole's products)

• • •

Eating out should never pose a serious problem. In restaurants you can order broiled fish, meat or poultry, a vegetable or two, and salad, fresh fruit and decaffeinated coffee, to have a perfect meal. When you are invited to a friend's house and are not sure what the hostess will be serving, eat a broiled hamburger and have a glass of milk before leaving home. Then, at table, take little and invent excuses, and try to push the items around your plate if necessary; the salad or the vegetables often are all right; and for dessert there may be fruit. When traveling, prepare snacks and juices to take along.

When entertaining at home, you can prepare dinner for yours guests and not have to feel that you are serving food fit for sick people. Your meal can be as exciting and appetizing as the best of them. Don't apologize or even discuss your food problem. Prepare and serve and —enjoy. They will. Many people are on special diets today. So you never have to get into any hassle about yours. If anyone asks you about your funny food desires, just tell them this is your "thing." Everyone has a thing today anyway.

Remember that many of these recipes are a compromise. For example, the absence of sugar and wheat flour will affect texture, taste and appearance of certain desserts. But don't worry. I have served many of the desserts to friends, and they never really knew they were eating something special. So the compromise is usually very slight.

In general, don't make a fuss about the whole approach to cooking and eating this new way; it really is not different from any other type (except gourmet cooking). Everyone has his own preference when it comes to food. Just cook with a light hand, season well and think about how attractive you can make it look.

And keep in mind that the recipes in this book are offered as a guide, not as set rules. Be inventive. You may use more or less of the artificial sweeteners; you may season foods to your personal taste. If you can improve a recipe in any way, do so—and let me know about it!

Index

ABOUT THE AUTHOR

Francyne Davis lives in New York City and for more than ten years has been a pioneer in making both the public and the medical profession better aware of the nature and the extent of hypoglycemia. She has been active in the Hypoglycemia Foundation and other organizations.

The Low Blood Sugar Cookbook

is a varied and imaginative collection of personally tested, mouth-watering recipes for nutritious eating. More than a cookbook catering to low blood sugar sufferers, it's a valuable guide for weight watchers and problem eaters. It boasts recipes so appetizing that gourmets will vie for its secrets. Stop tantalizing yourself as your friends eat outrageous desserts and breads. With this cookbook in hand you, too, can enjoy such palate-pleasers as Strawberry Bavarian Cream, Manicotti, Spicy Beef Roast, Chicken Provençal, Lemon Cheesecake, Hot Spiced Apple Punch and many more. There are over two hundred scrumptious low-sugar, low-starch recipes — from spreads, dips, cheese and eggs to vegetables, desserts and beverages. Your dieting, weight-conscious friends will be more than willing dinner guests.